MOVING FROM STRENGTH

SPECIAL NEEDS CAREGIVERS

by
Mara Boughton, M.Ed.

Copyright © 2021 by Mara Boughton

Published by Xavier Patrick Books

All rights reserved. No part of this book may be reproduced or used in any manner without written permission of the copyright owner except for the use of quotations in a book review. For more information, please contact: livingthespecialneedslife@gmail.com

FIRST EDITION
Paperback ISBN: 978-1-7367543-0-6
Ebook ISBN: 978-1-7367543-1-3

https://livingthespecialneedslife.com/
Cover Design by Martin Dunn
featuring textures by
Eddi van W - https://tinyurl.com/mvtk927f

MOVING FROM STRENGTH

SPECIAL NEEDS CAREGIVERS

CONTENTS

Author's Note—xiii
Doers and Dreamers —1
Forward—4
Introduction —12
Panic at the Diagnosis—16
Meet Billy—20
The Medical Questions—23
Meet Lisa—25
You and Your Child Are OK—28
Meet Julia—33
Mourning—38
It's All Been Done Before—40
Meet John & Martina—42
Pressure—45
Checking Your Stress at The Baggage Check—48
Follow Your Gut—52

Follow-Up to Follow Your Gut—61

Crafting Your Special Needs Life —65

Avoid Burnout —71

Changing Your Inner Dialogue for Success —77

How to Identify Assets and Liabilities —82

Moving from Strength, not Fear—87

No One Has It All Figured Out—93

Post-Traumatic Growth When Living the Special Needs Life – It's a Thing—97

Why Streamlining is Important—102

A Setback Doesn't Have to Be a Downfall—106

This is the Greatest Time in History for Your Child with Special Needs to Be Alive—110

Afterward—114

How You Can Help—115

About the Author—116

ACKNOWLEDGMENTS

For my mother in heaven. Hey, Mom, look what I made!

For Edlin, who told me that if I was struggling in writing the forward because it included the story of my mother's death, that I didn't have to do it alone. That we could make a time to sit on the floor at CrossFit, order pizza and just let me write and cry, while everyone sat around me being supportive. I'll never forget when you said that.

For Michelle, who did it first and did it well. Thanks for showing me that it could be done!

For Q. For everything.

For all of the teachers, doctors, nurses, nurse practitioners, therapists, teaching assistants, parent support advocates, principals and EVERYONE who has touched our lives in the ongoing care of Kai. You guys rock!

For those who agreed, as special needs caregivers, to be

interviewed for this book. Going back through all of the memories and experiences can be painful but also reminds us of just how far we have come!

For my inner circle. Ya'll know who you are.

For my older kids, Autum, Ace, and Summer (my choice kids). You accepted Kai and his differences from the very beginning. You loved him and continue to love him as he is. You have no idea what that means to me.

For Jason, Meagan & Austin, my older kids' partners. You accepted and loved Kai and I love you for it.

For Amaya. My birth daughter, the best big sister ever. I waited my whole life to meet you and can't imagine my life without you. I love you!

For Billy, my husband, my partner. You were OK before I was OK. You led me by example and showed me that the new normal was not only going to be OK but amazing. I was right behind you but you were there first. You make me proud every single day.

For Kai. I set out to make your sister, Amaya, a little sister to grow up with. I got a boy with special needs. Turns out, you were exactly what I wanted. I am so glad that you are mine.

For special needs caregivers everywhere. When I first became a special needs caregiver, I looked around for a book like this and couldn't find one. So I wrote one. I hope that it gives you peace, a sense of direction and most importantly, the knowledge that you are OK.

AUTHOR'S NOTE

YOU MAY FIND that there are some inconsistencies in the order of this book. For example, there are times when you will first read that my son, Kai, is eight years old. At other times, he is said to be seven or six years old. This is because it took two years to write everything, being interrupted the whole way (such is life!). I have left the age listed because at the time of the writing, it was accurate. Thanks for understanding.

DOERS AND DREAMERS

The difference between doers and dreamers is action...

Everyone has dreams...

Not everyone makes their dreams come true...

YOU are a doer...

You dream the dream, make the plan, work the plan, fall down, pick yourself back up and you fall again...

You cry and sweat and suffer and ask yourself, "Who am I to think that I could be a doer?"

But you are who everyone else wants to be...

They watch you and they say that you are LUCKY...

Because you have what they think that they want...

You do what they wish they could do...

And they don't understand that they, too, could do it, just like you...

If only...

2   Moving from Strength

If only it wasn't so much work... as you work...

If only it wasn't so intimidating... as you overcome...

If only it didn't require risk... as you risk...

If only it wouldn't make them fall down so that they had to pick themselves up... as you fall down...

If only they could feel the fear and do it anyway... as you feel fear and do it anyway...

If only it didn't require them to fail spectacularly over and over, until the day they finally succeed... as you have failed and then succeeded...

Doers know that it is all about the journey, the sweat, the stamina and the sacrifice...

Dreamers only see your success and say, I wish someone would hand this to me as it has been handed to you...

They don't understand... that the person who hands it to you is yourself...

As a person who wants to become a runner becomes one by lacing up their shoes and just going for their first run...

As a person who wants to become a musician becomes one by picking up their instrument and playing their first notes...

As a person who wants to become a blogger becomes one by getting on their computer and beginning to write their first blog...

As a person who wants to become a karate master becomes one by putting on their white belt and taking their first class...

A DOER becomes A DOER by DOING...
YOU are a DOER.
You SHINE.

FORWARD

LIFE DOESN'T STOP when you have a child with special needs. You would think that when something like this occurs, the world would accommodate you by slowing everything else down to give you time to acclimate, get your feet under you, and give things a whirl.

Nope.

This was especially true in our case. In 2012, I excitedly gave birth to my son, Kai. He was seemingly perfect, like his sister, Amaya, born two years before. But right around this time, all hell broke loose in our lives.

My mother finally admitted to me, after months of me trying to figure out what was wrong, that she had been diagnosed with Alzheimer's Disease. She had been hiding this from me for TWO YEARS. But, as her disease progressed, she was no longer able to hide it; her behavior was becoming increasingly weirder. Strange. We were living in Texas, I was pregnant, and my mother was sick with a long-term illness and living in Las Vegas, Nevada. I flew there, eight-plus months pregnant, in January 2012, to make a game plan.

My mother didn't want to move. She flat-out refused. She had friends there, had a home there and she was staying there. What does a daughter do when facing this situation? My husband and I, and ALL FIVE OF OUR KIDS, as well as our son-in-law and new baby grandson, picked up and moved to Las Vegas to be with her. When we moved (we drove, because things should be as difficult as possible), Kai was four months old. He was a seemingly perfect, happy baby.

We all moved into a huge new house together, got settled in and I got a job teaching ESL pre-K at a local public school. My husband, bless him, stayed home and took care of the house, our kids, and my mother. He took her to every doctor's appointment, managed her medicine and was a rock star. He also took Kai to his wellness checkups and it was he who was informed that Kai was not advancing as he should. We were referred to Early Childhood Intervention Services. They said he appeared autistic, but some characteristics made them question whether this was correct, including the fact that Kai could hold eye contact well. He was referred for an MRI. Kudos to that doctor because most kids never get an MRI in this situation. We found out that Kai had periventricular leukomalacia (PVL), a rare diagnosis, often misdiagnosed as autism. This is a brain injury. Kai had damaged white brain matter. We were stunned. We wanted to know why.

Sometimes in the world of special needs, you don't ever get to know why. No one knows the cause of PVL but it is thought that a lack of oxygen to the brain can cause the damage. Often, this can be the result of being born prematurely, infection, drug or alcohol use by the mother, and more. But none of these things were present in our history. Kai has PVL. We don't know why.

Remember, my mother was also deteriorating during this time. She was a Harvard educated college psychologist who could no longer put on her own seatbelt and bit me as a joke when I did it for her. Hard. She couldn't dress herself, forgot how to use utensils when eating and, as time went on, palmed her meds and began to run from one piece of furniture to the other, trying to outrun her disease. Add in our moving to a new state, a new job for me, my husband being caught in this situation without respite, our two-year-old (Kai's older sister) and all of our other kids and new grandson and let me tell you, it was stressful.

Kai, happy no matter what was going on, thank goodness, needed intense therapy in all areas. The therapists started coming to the house for as many as seven sessions a week. Speech, OT, PT, Feeding and more. He would choke on baby food to the point of needing intervention every single day. My husband became scared to feed him when

I wasn't there because what if this was the time where we couldn't clear his air passages?

But with all of this, Kai made strides. Literally. At 22 months, he walked for the first time. He took three steps the first day. The next day he took 35 steps. After a year of intense therapy, he was able to swallow food without choking. Still baby food, but we were beyond thrilled.

And my mother was failing. She spent a week in the hospital with gastrointestinal issues, only for me to discover later that she was secretly eating a bar of pretty, handmade soap she had hidden in her room, thinking it was candy. She had an alert system attached to her hospital bed so in case she tried to get up, it would alert the nurses. My mother had nothing else to do but lay there, so she worked until she dismantled the whole system. She completely took it apart. We tried a rehab center and after one night, where she worked the entire staff to exhaustion, they asked us to come and get her.

My mother stopped eating and drinking altogether. We had to carry her out the front door of the house, feet first, screaming all the way back to the hospital. At the hospital entrance, my husband went in to get help and left us alone. I turned and looked at my mother in the back seat. She was so tired and glazed. I said, "Mom, here's the thing. You are not eating and drinking. You have a DNR. If you don't start to eat and drink, you are going to die. What do you want to do?"

My mother, my best friend in the world, my champion, looked me right in the eyes. Her glazed expression seemed to clear. She said, in a strong voice with conviction, "I want to die."

I took a deep breath. "OK, Mom. OK."

We spent the next five days in hospice. I made sure that she was medicated and felt no pain. She was comfortable. I watched over her, and on the fifth evening, she passed away.

Still, life didn't stop. This was March. Our family was now living in Las Vegas, with no purpose for being there. We had uprooted our entire lives to care for my mother, thinking it would be a ten-year ordeal because these things supposedly go slowly. We were there for two years. I finished out the school year, we cleaned up the house, sorted her things, and put the house on the market to head home to Texas, which is where we had originally decided our lives would be. So we flew to Texas, picked out a house, put in an offer and flew back to Las Vegas. The offer was accepted.

We started investigating therapy opportunities for Kai near the new house as we packed the old one. We got Kai's file of medical information together and we moved. We were driving, yet again. On the second day of our three day drive, we were informed that the deal had fallen through. The sellers had backed out, no reason given. And now, we were homeless.

We lived in a long-term hotel for three months while we house hunted. The stress was unbelievable. Kai, of course, took it all in stride, happy to be with his family, doing whatever we were doing. He was two years old now, not interested in toys, books or any of the usual stuff two-year-olds like. But he did like music and being sung to. Also, any child shows with music made him happy. And anything knitted or crocheted such as a blanket or sweater made him happy. Not stuffed animals, though. Kai had definite likes and dislikes.

We finally got into a new home. We found new therapists for Kai. They were not as good as the ones in Las Vegas, but our time with Early Childhood Intervention was coming to an end soon anyway, as Kai was turning three. He would be eligible for special-ed pre-K starting the day after his third birthday until he was five. And when we transitioned, we were beyond blessed to get a teacher and assistant teachers who were truly excellent.

Kai got more therapy. Massive amounts of repetition was how Kai learned. Hundreds of repetitions. We were exhausted but it was working. Kai was getting it. Yes, he was low-functioning and non-verbal. But he was happy (noticing a happiness pattern?).

Think life stopped and gave us a chance to catch our breath? Nope.

Kai was continuously diagnosed. PVL, yes, but he also had Duplicate Chromosome 16 (both of these diagnoses were rare versions). And autism. Sensory processing disorder. Apraxia. Delays in all areas, including speech, PT, OT. Low functioning. The hits just kept coming (did I mention how happy he was?).

Then my husband got sick. Non-alcoholic fatty liver disease. Hepatitis. He almost died twice. This was 2017 and he is still in recovery as of now, Spring 2020. These were some rocky years to say the least. Kai moved out of special-ed pre-K and into special-ed Kindergarten and to a teacher who was inept and that's putting it kindly. Things weren't going well.

So, we moved again. Our older kids (my step kids, his birth kids), lived two hours away. We had no one to help us and I needed help. You can't just leave a low-functioning special needs child with an average babysitter and our older kids knew what Kai needed. They could help me when their dad needed me to be at the hospital. So we moved to East Texas.

And now, finally, the world has stopped and given us a break (you know, except for the pandemic, but that's a whole other story). Kai found a home in his new school, which he absolutely adores. It is a small, all special-needs campus (no inclusion for him, that would never work). The teachers, assistants, secretary, principal, bus drivers… everyone is absolutely amazing. We have downsized and live in a small home in the woods. We didn't have to go this small but it eases finances and lets us focus on more important things. My husband has a long road to recovery but is making progress. My daughter, Amaya, now ten, loves her new school and is making straight A's while taking the gaming world by storm. Our older kids live nearby, each having made us grandparents.

Deep. Breath.

This is our story. While it may be crazier than yours, I am not telling it to make you feel bad about your feelings regarding your own situation. It doesn't at all lessen what you are going through. It is to let you know that I know that life has not stopped because your child has gotten a special needs diagnosis. My mother, when she was whole, once said, "Just because the person next to you has two broken legs, doesn't mean your one broken leg doesn't hurt." I know it's hard. It was unforeseen. You never envisioned your life this way. Who does?

I want you to know that Kai is OK. In fact, he may be one of the happiest kids in the world! I am OK. My husband is OK. And the rest of our kids and grandkids are OK. Even after all of that.

You will be OK too.

When it was happening to me, I needed someone to tell me that. I am so glad that you decided to pick up this book. I hope it gives you comfort and direction to a place where you feel OK. It is the book I wish that someone had handed me upon that first diagnosis for Kai. No one handed it to me. I couldn't find it. So I wrote it.

XOXO,

Mara

INTRODUCTION
WHEN THINGS ARE BEYOND YOUR CONTROL

We all know on some level that having control is an illusion. The fact is most of what happens in the world is beyond our control. We make daily choices, of course, but many, many things happen TO us. And so, sometimes, as we get older, we become more compliant than we should. We think, well, that is just how things are. That is how the system works. This is what has always been done. And as long as we feel that we have some personal choices, we tend to feel OK.

And then something comes along that is beyond our control that shakes us up. Something that we never imagined. That we never saw coming. And suddenly, we no longer feel OK.

Like discovering that your child has special needs.

I have never, I mean NEVER, in all of the many times

I've met other parents and caregivers of children with special needs, met one who said they originally envisioned their child would be atypical. The only exception to this is someone who deliberately chose to adopt a child with special needs. But those incredible, amazing people are not who I'm talking to right now (of course, they are invited to read on!). I'm talking to YOU FOLKS.

You envision having a family, getting pregnant (or having a pregnant partner) and having a child who is TYPICAL. That is your expectation. I mean, who doesn't expect that? And in all of your wildest dreams of parenting – diapers, formula, breastfeeding, potty training, school choices, cute clothes, teaching them sports or to dance, prom, college, THEIR wedding, grandchildren – you never think JTUBE. Or AUTISM. Or DYSLEXIA. Or PERIVENTRICULAR LEUKOMALACIA (How do you like that one? It took me 18 months to be able to spell it after my son was diagnosed with it. And I consider myself an excellent speller.).

And, suddenly, you feel an incredible loss of control.

Panic? Let's talk about panic. As in, WHAT THE HELL DO I DO NOW? As in, WHY IS THIS HAPPENING TO ME? As in, I DON'T EVEN KNOW HOW TO PARENT A TYPICAL CHILD YET, HOW AM I GOING TO DO THIS? As in, I AM SO IN LOVE WITH MY NEW BABY BUT WHAT DO I DO ABOUT THE FACT THAT HE/SHE ALSO TERRIFIES ME? As in, NO ONE IN MY FAMILY HAS ANY EXPERIENCE WITH A CHILD

LIKE MINE AND THEY WERE THE ONES WHO WERE SUPPOSED TO HELP ME!

Here comes the deer in the headlights, the shortness of breath, wanting to burst into tears, feeling like you were caught and got in trouble for something you didn't do.

Guess what?

Your response is NORMAL.

The helplessness. The loss of control. The new path that you didn't envision. The feeling there is a lack of guidance, that you are feeling your way in the darkness. The PRESSURE that this is the most important person in your life and YOU are the one who will have to guide how their life goes and YOU HAVE NO IDEA WHAT YOU ARE DOING AND O...M...G!!!!!!

Yup. Normal.

The truth of the matter is that nothing was ever guaranteed. You didn't have any control over if your child was going to be typical or atypical (leaving lifestyle choices during pregnancy out of it). It was never within your control.

But you want to know what IS within your control? What happens next.

That's what this book is all about. Where do you go from here?

It may feel like your child has become two entities. What you ENVISIONED AND BECAME ATTACHED TO as you waited for your child to be born – typical, "whole," "normal." And who your child REALLY IS – atypical, but still "whole," still "normal" for them.

The child you envisioned, who you became attached to, who you had plans for and have dreamed about – that version of your child didn't come to fruition. THEY DON'T EXIST. And that can feel like a HUGE loss.

This is a loss that will take time, that will need to be mourned. We are going to talk about mourning: The loss of the child you envisioned, and the child who is here now, your REAL child, who needs and DESERVES all of you.

We are going to talk about how to regain your perception of control. How to feel OK again.

We are going to talk about what your new normal could possibly look like.

We are going to talk about what you can expect from the people you have considered to be your inner circle for what may be a long, long time. And how their reactions may not be what you would think. And that this is OK.

We are off on a wild adventure, you and I. I know you are shocked. I know you are afraid. But it is going to be OK.

I PROMISE.

Keep reading and you'll see.

PANIC AT THE DIAGNOSIS

Nothing could have prepared you for this moment. Your child, the one you have planned for and dreamed about and celebrated, is NOT "NORMAL." You may be a first time parent or a fifth time parent but either way, suddenly you are a deer in headlights. As in, HOLY CRAP! And the questions start rolling through your mind:

Are they sure?
Why my child?
Why me?
Why us?
What does this mean?
Will my life ever be the same again?
How in the world am I going to do this?
Is it possible that they are wrong?
Is this a misdiagnosis?
Did that one glass of wine I had before I knew I was

pregnant have anything to do with this?

Is my child going to be in that special class that I always saw going down the hallways when I was in school?

Will I love my child like I would have if they were "normal?"

What if I can't do this?

What if I don't want to do this?

What if I love them but I can't tell if they love me?

What do these diagnosis words that I have never heard of before mean?

If I make a mistake, could my child die?

If my child is high functioning, will they get bullied at school because they seem "normal" but don't fit in?

Will we ever go anywhere as a family again?

How are the grandparents going to feel when they find out that I gave them a grandchild who isn't "normal?"

How will I take my child out in public when I feel like everyone will be staring at me?

What if my child disrupts everything if I take them out in public?

While there are THOUSANDS of questions that might go through our minds at the first diagnosis, and even before that, at the first notice of difference, one of the biggest, most common questions we ask ourselves is: "Is this my fault?"

Every situation is different. While I can't comment on whether or not this was your fault (or your partner's, the environment, the food you ate, whether or not you drank alcohol, did drugs, have something that runs in your bloodline), I can say that I know that it is tempting to think about it and wonder. For many, many of us, we will just never know why our child is different than the typical child. There is ABSOLUTELY NO REASON why my son ended up being a kid who has eight different diagnoses THAT WE ARE AWARE OF. We know what the diagnoses are but we don't know why he has them. And don't think we haven't tried to figure it out. We've read the books, studied online and asked the experts.

Is there an actual reason? I'm sure there is. And every now and then I will ponder, again, this mystery. But you need to decide how much time you want to devote to this because it can eat up time like nobody's business.

It is what it is. This is one of my least favorite expressions in the world. But there you go. Believe me when I tell you the endless amount of time you could be/are spending on this could be better used by taking care of your child. And yourself.

As for all of the other questions listed above, and more, you can rank them in order of importance. The most important one though, the thing you need to know as soon as possible, is what, if any, medical care issues need to be addressed RIGHT NOW. The second most important thing is to establish what other care needs must be addressed (i.e. establishing home routines, educational path if old enough, etc.) Finally, the third most important thing to address on this list is to breathe and know that if it's not an emergency, you have time to work things out. Some things you will have to figure out on your own and other things will just reveal themselves to you over time.

If emergency care is established or not needed and general care is rolling, then you are OK. And your child is OK.

MEET BILLY

Father to: Kai

Billy's age at Kai's diagnosis: 39

Kai's Age at Diagnosis: 14 months

Kai's Diagnoses: periventricular leukomalacia (PVL), duplicate chromosome 16, autism, sensory processing disorder, apraxia, coprophagia, developmental delays in all areas, history of feeding issues, seizures

On Having a Background with Special Needs People Before Having Kai:

I grew up with a mother who worked with people with MHMR. All throughout my childhood, kids from the state school would be guests at our house. Eventually, when I grew up, I became an officer at the school. I also was in a long-term relationship with a woman who had a son with special needs (MS/MHMR) who I cared for. I was very comfortable with people with special needs and not at all afraid when we discovered that Kai was different. I have yet to meet another parent who said that they weren't afraid when their child was diagnosed. But I just wasn't.

On Feeling Like Kai Was a Gift from God:

Ultimately, I feel that I did something somewhere along the way that showed God that I was worthy of being given the gift of Kai because he knew that I could handle it. He was meant for us, me and my wife and family. And we were meant for him. I feel honored that I get to be his role model and help guide him. To be his forever protector.

On What Has Gotten Harder Over Time:

I was sick with a long-term illness for the last several years. Not being able to care for him like I wanted to was really hard. I am so grateful that I am getting my health back and able to be much more hands on now. But this has also driven the point home that our mortality (mine and my wife's) is a real issue. I want us to take care of Kai forever and I know that we will eventually die. And that is really hard.

On What Has Gotten Easier Over Time:

Communicating with Kai and figuring out his wants and needs is getting easier as he learns some words and signs. Also, he has moved on from an entire year of choking at every meal which was very stressful – I would think every day, what if this is the one where we can't clear the food out and he dies? It was terrifying. I am so glad that period is over.

On What It Is About Kai that Makes Him Amazing:

Everything! His smile, his laughter, when he dances with his Mommy and looks into her eyes with so much love. His stubbornness, his mischievousness. The spark in his eyes. His love for life. Kai has no cares in the world. He brings joy to everyone around him.

THE MEDICAL QUESTIONS - WHEN IT'S A COMMON DIAGNOSIS (AND WHEN IT'S NOT)

I AM GOING to leave the medical questions to the medical professionals. However, I will tell you this: the great majority of diagnoses have been seen before. How you choose to handle it, along with handling the advice of the professionals you have and are going to be consulting with, is up to you. Your child is unique in that no one else is them but in all likelihood, their diagnosis probably isn't (if it is, I will address that in a little while. My son's diagnosis WAS unusual. Hey, it happens).

Why is it a comfort to know your child's diagnosis has been seen before? Because it means you don't have to reinvent the wheel. You can breathe a sigh of relief, knowing that the pressure isn't on you to figure out from scratch how to handle what comes next. Instead, you can:

1. Ask the person who diagnosed your child what the

next steps are.

2. Ask for a referral to a parent support group (PLEASE DON'T SKIP THIS STEP, YOU NEED THIS).

3. Ask for referrals to competent professionals who are experienced in the area of your child's diagnosis.

4. Make the phone calls and contacts necessary to set up the appointments needed to get your child situated.

5. TAKE A BREAK. COLLAPSE. IT IS TIME TO REFLECT, REEVALUATE and RETHINK.

For those of you who have an unusual diagnosis, it can be unsettling when the doctor you are consulting with has that same "deer in the headlights" look you see in your own eyes when you look in the mirror. If they are not familiar with what your child has and they TELL you, you have found a gem. You want someone to be honest with you and not throw you a bunch of B.S. to save face because "the doctor knows all" (You will discover, quickly, they don't always know all).

Find an expert. If it is so unusual that there isn't one, or isn't one local, try to figure out a diagnosis that is SIMILAR to what your child has and go from there and find an expert in THAT. Don't be afraid to call famous hospitals and teaching hospitals anywhere in the world because, yes, your child is important! Then go back and again, follow the steps above.

MEET LISA

Mother to: Austin
Lisa's age at Austin's diagnosis: 34
Austin's Age at Diagnosis: Late Age 2 to Early Age 3
Austin's Diagnosis: Autism

On Her Feelings When She Noticed Differences and Then at Diagnosis:

I thought it wouldn't add up to mean anything. That he is doing some "odd" things but he will grow out of it. My spouse thought the same thing, that everything will be ok. It won't equal a diagnosis. And especially nothing like Autism. We were concerned, but not overly concerned. All kids develop differently and my child was no exception. And we still thought nothing is probably wrong. "He's a boy, they develop slower than girls." That's what we said to ourselves.

So there was no spiritual, mental, or physical feelings at that time. How did I feel at diagnosis? Horrible!!! Many, many, many tears. I couldn't say the word "autism" for a long time. We felt like we were experiencing a loss. A loss of what we had pictured for our son's future. So many questions, so much uncertainty. I felt defeat spiritually, mentally, and physically. I cried so much I am sure my tears added up to at least 5 gallons. I couldn't and didn't want to talk to anyone except for my husband about this diagnosis. We didn't tell anyone except the grandparents about the diagnosis. Anyone else would have to find out themselves, conducting their own observations because I wasn't discussing it.

On What Has Gotten Harder Over Time:

I certainly do give more thought to my child's ability to support himself, live on his own, get married, have children, and live an independent and fulfilling life as he gets older. I'm not sure if he is going to be employable. And all of the above has me very concerned.

On What Has Gotten Easier Over Time:

Being able to talk about autism, being able to say the word "autism," being able to accept that autism is part of my son's life and my family's life. Just accepting autism.

On What You Fear Most on Your Journey:

I fear that I will die before I can fully raise my children, before giving them all the knowledge I can to make them successful adults.

On Handling Self-Care:

Am I good at self-care? I would have to say yes and no. Yes, I take care of the physical. I have weekly hair appointments, biweekly nail appointments and pedicures. I travel with and without my family. But I could do better taking care of the "inner me." Get more sleep, drink more water, slow down, take more deep breaths, enjoy the scenery more. I think I am not good at that because I don't take the time to be good at it. Sometimes I am too focused on the task and I forget to enjoy the journey. I also have so much going on, I don't want to give up any of the projects I am juggling.

On What It Is About Austin That Makes Him Amazing:

Austin is very kind and in tune with other individual's feelings. He is really concerned about other people. He's always there to tell others "it will be ok, don't worry." He is extremely thoughtful, i.e. if he notices I am squinting, he finds my glasses for me. He just notices so much around him.

YOU AND YOUR CHILD ARE OK

Having a child with special needs isn't the end of the world. In fact, it is the opening up of a new world that you are about to step into and experience as an insider. If you think of the fact that EVERYONE has special needs in one form or another, this concept can be less scary.

So…what kind of special needs does the average person have?

- Some people can't sleep well.

- Some people are night people and can only function well then.

- Some people can only hold a conversation if you turn off the television. If you leave it on, they can't focus when their attention is split between the T.V. and the person they are talking to.

- Some people can only learn by doing while following

instructions. Other people can only learn by watching. Then there are still other people who can only learn by ignoring instructions, jumping in and figuring it out for themselves.

- Some people can only ride in a car if they are the ones who are driving.

- Some people are VERY introverted and need lots of alone time. Then, when they interact with others, it can be excruciatingly painful.

But, you say, these are NOT special needs! These are NORMAL things that people have issues with.

On the contrary, these are special needs that are so common, people just call them needs. Or quirks.

Special needs become "special" simply because they are less common. And maybe it causes folks to need more help. More care. If your child has been diagnosed with "special needs," their needs are less common than the "average" kid's needs.

That's it.

Of course, this can make them look wildly different. I don't mean to belittle that. You know what I mean?

You are OK. Your child is OK. Your family is also OK. This is not what you envisioned. And that's hard, isn't it? I'm not going to tell you that it's not hard, because I know it is. It's scary to head straight into the unknown as the LEADER in the situation when you have no idea what you are doing. You didn't volunteer for this job.

You didn't sign up for this gig. Or did you?

Let's forget about the special needs for a moment, let's focus instead on your child. Take a good look at them. Put this book down, right now, and take a gander. Really see your child. And come back to me after you've looked.

Are you back? Good. Now let's talk about what you DID sign up for. Because it's still there. When you decided to become a parent, you signed up for:

- a lifetime connection

- the opportunity to shower another human being, one you call your own from birth, with love and affection

- the job of being this new human being's guide in the world and introducing them to all of the cool new experiences to be had

- the opportunity to be this new person's protector

- a lifetime of care (because we all know that it doesn't stop at age 18)

None of this has changed. What has changed is that your child with special needs is going to need a bit more of everything. And just like with a "normal" child, where you may have to study up on geometry to help them when they reach that level in school, you are going to have to study up on this curveball that has been thrown to you early in the game – the diagnosis. Because your child has reached this early in their game of life, if you are not knowledgeable about what they need, you are going to have to gather information and become knowledgeable so you can help them. Just like if they needed help with geometry.

NO ONE EXPECTS YOU TO KNOW WHAT YOU ARE DOING when your child first gets a special needs diagnosis.

I have a master's degree in education and taught in the general education classroom for fifteen years. I am ESL certified (which means I can teach students when English is their second language) and am what is called "highly qualified." I did not, in any way, feel competent when my son's diagnoses started rolling in. Check out this list for my son:

- Periventricular Leukomalacia (PVL)
- Duplicate Chromosome 16
- Autism
- Sensory Processing Disorder
- Apraxia
- Developmental Delays in All Areas
- Feeding Issues (including daily choking at EVERY meal requiring intervention on my part for an ENTIRE YEAR)
- Seizures

All I can say is, thank goodness the diagnoses didn't all come at the same time – I might have had a nervous breakdown!

I want to tell you something. I am OK. My son is OK. And my family is OK. I certainly didn't feel that way when I realized something was different about my son and I DEFINITELY didn't feel that way when this was verified by diagnosis after diagnosis, but we WERE and ARE OK.

There is a learning curve. Especially when you get a diagnosis like periventricular leukomalacia. I couldn't pronounce it for the first year and I couldn't spell it for almost two years, let alone explain what it was. No one I knew had ever heard of it. Heck, most DOCTORS hadn't heard of it. But my son is still my son. He has an incredible smile that lights up the world. And nothing, not a single thing in this whole world, including a list of diagnoses longer than my arm, can change that. Simply NOTHING.

We are OK. And so are you. You may not feel OK right now. But you are. And soon you will feel that way, too. Stay with me, it's going to get better.

MEET JULIA

Mother to: Nicholas

Julia's age at Nicolas' diagnosis: 31

Nicholas' age at Diagnosis: 5.5 months

Nicholas' Diagnoses: Translocation between 2nd and 18th chromosomes, epilepsy, severe developmental delays, some skeletal issues with his hip and back.

On Her Experience with Special Needs Before Having Her Child:

I am embarrassed to say that I was always afraid of people with special needs. I grew up in the 1960's and most often special needs children were placed in state run institutions so exposure to people with special needs was limited. In fact, there were two families with special needs children on our block and I only saw one of the children from one family. The other family had two or three children with special needs and I never met them once. There was a man with Down's Syndrome named Larry who was not institutionalized and would hang out at the local park. As a child, I was terrified of him and avoided him at all costs. About 25 years later my high school named him Homecoming King. I wish I knew then what I know now.

On Her Reaction Upon Realization Her Child Was Different:

Terror. Nick was age appropriate until about four months. After his 2nd DPT (1991) he began losing milestones and would have little rhythmic jerks that would sometimes last for an hour or more. I was very concerned and voiced my concerns to my then mother-in-law who had been raised Christian Scientist. She and my father-in-law kept telling me that I was an overly anxious, first-time mom. On the flip side, my parents were both in medicine and were also very concerned. At the time I was living in Arizona and my family was in Minnesota. The night before Nick's doctor's appointment my father-in-law told me I should cancel the appointment because there was nothing wrong with Nick. I almost cancelled the appointment but decided I needed to know what was going on.

On Physical, Mental, Emotional, and Spiritual Feelings:

I was drained in all four areas and I was in denial. I knew something was wrong and was worried sick but it didn't cross my mind that what was going on might be a sign of something much bigger and more permanent.

On Her Feelings at Diagnosis:

I had taken Nick to the pediatrician alone and against the wishes of my in-laws. At that point, I thought I was insane and that what I was seeing may be normal behavior (at least I wanted to believe that I WAS just an anxious parent but I didn't think I was) so when I was in the waiting room and Nick began his rhythmic, tiny little jerks I asked the receptionist to come and watch him so she could help me describe it to the doctor. She then went and got a nurse to watch with me. When we saw the pediatrician, she was incredibly kind and reassuring that "we" would figure out what was going on. I am sure she knew something was up because she left the room and, when she came back, she had us booked into a neurologist that afternoon. I felt huge relief because in my mind we were going to finally figure this out, get some medicine and all would be okay.

Then we saw the neurologist.

Just as in the pediatrician's office, Nick began jerking in the waiting room and again, I asked the receptionist to watch with me. She went and got the doctor. He came out to the waiting room and said that even if I had just described the behavior to him, he would have known what was going on. Again, big relief for me as I thought that now we were finally getting closer to my baby getting better. He took us back to the exam room and he measured Nick's head and asked me all kinds of questions and then gave me the news. "Nick has infantile spasms and will be somewhere in the moderate to severe category of mental retardation. The best-case scenario is that someday he may be able to have some kind of small job." I sat, smile frozen on my face, thinking "this guy doesn't know what the fuck he is talking about." The next day was Saturday and he lined up an EEG at his office. After that, he confirmed the diagnosis.

I was devastated, my husband was devastated and my in-laws were, too, but they never once validated me or my "anxious, first-time parent" hunch.

In addition, when the neurologist had given me the news, he told me that Nick would need ACTH injections and the side effects would cause Nick to quit sleeping and be fussy and cry a lot. I brought up my Christian Scientist based in-laws and we developed a plan whereby I could take Nick and fly back to Minneapolis for treatment should they try to stop me. I knew my family would be completely on board with the medications but I wasn't sure about my husband's parents. [But] they posed no problem when they realized the seriousness of Nick's illness.

On Who Was "On Board" with the Situation:

I do have to say that everyone was "on board" with our situation. My mother-in-law would take Nick for an overnight each week (the ACTH gave him horrible insomnia) and she was quite comforting. My mom came to visit from Minneapolis and was wonderful. The ACTH stripped Nick of his immunities so we didn't want sitters or anyone really, who could bring in a cold or the flu so we were on our own a lot.

On What Has Gotten Harder Over Time:

As I've gotten older, I worry more about Nick's living situation after I die. At the moment, he lives with his father and step-mother and has a wonderful set-up and is out in the community every day. He has been in two group homes before and neither gave Nick the care his father and I want for him. Nick is incredibly social and needs to be out and about. At the group homes, TV was the most prevalent activity.

On What Has Gotten Easier:

Nick's dad and I had a very challenging relationship for about the first 25 years of Nick's life. We struggled to balance care for Nick after we separated. That has now improved. Also, Nick has grown up and isn't the hitting, biting, scratching person he used to be. When the threat of physical injury is removed, it's much easier to have a good time with Nick. It is always awful when Nick sabotages his own outing with behaviors; now that is a rare occurrence.

On How You Find Respite When You Need It:

Nick doesn't live with me, he is 6'3" and heavy so I really cannot do a lot of his daily care. Living with his dad affords me the luxury of seeing Nick on my own terms.

MOURNING

You had a vision. You were having a baby. You became a parent. And then the rug was seemingly pulled out from under you.

Whether you knew about the special needs in utero, at birth, when your child was very young or you didn't find out until much later, it is still a loss. While we are SO GRATEFUL for the child we have, now we have to let go of the child we envisioned.

Maybe you envisioned a child who could hear and your child has hearing loss. Maybe you envisioned having a child who could walk and your child will be on crutches or in a wheelchair for the rest of their life. Maybe you envisioned that your child would grow and develop mentally at a typical rate and your actual child might NEVER get beyond the mental age of a toddler. Or maybe your child is developing normally but absolutely cannot sit still or pay attention in any way without medication.

The child that you envisioned is gone. The fact that they never really existed doesn't erase the loss that you feel. And many of us feel guilty. We are secretly upset. We are mourning a child when our child is right here with us. But we don't know how to explain this to other people, especially those who are not special needs caregivers. How can we mourn a child who never existed?

We look at our own children and feel even more guilty. We want to accept them wholeheartedly but it's so hard. And maybe we are angry. Maybe we want to know why. What did we do to deserve this path? What did our child do to deserve this path?

I want you to know that all of these feelings are normal. Mourning for the child you envisioned is normal. While you should take the time to mourn, to allow yourself to cry and let yourself feel these feelings, know that even if you think you have gotten through the mourning stage, it may come back when you least expect it. It comes and goes. And that's OK.

Try to allow these feelings. Take notice of them when you are feeling them. Know that they will pass. That you WILL recover. That you can be 100% there for your child, even while feeling these feelings.

You are not a bad person if you mourn for who you thought your child was going to be.

IT'S ALL BEEN DONE BEFORE

Observing difference and then getting diagnosis can be one of the most isolating experiences for parents and caregivers. This is VERY personal. Even though the diagnosis belongs to your child, the experience also belongs to YOU. It can feel like no one around you understands what you are going through. It feels new, it feels different and it feels lonely.

Imagine, though, that in a world filled with billions of people, even a rare diagnosis has usually been seen before, SOMEWHERE at SOME TIME. It is highly unlikely that your child's diagnosis is the first of its kind. And, even if it is (you trailblazers!), your caregiver experience most certainly has been done before. Whether you have a child with a physical disability, a cognitive disability, a combination of both or something outside of these boxes, YOU ARE NOT

ALONE IN THE WORLD WITH THIS EXPERIENCE.

There are all kinds of ways to handle your experience, to ease your burden, to make you feel OK again and get you acclimated to your new normal. Because, just like giving birth to a typical child, giving birth to a special needs child creates a new normal.

You knew that by having a child that nothing was ever going to be the same again. It is still true. When you have a typical child, EVERYTHING changes. When you have an atypical child, EVERYTHING STILL changes. It's just in a less predictable way.

The good news is that it becomes more predictable over time. As you get to know your child, get to know the different ways of doing things that work for them and become more familiar with what their diagnosis means, life will get simpler.

MEET JOHN & MARTINA

Parents to: Dale
John and Martina's ages at Dale's diagnosis: John 40, Martina 39
Dale's Age at Diagnosis: 4
Dale's Diagnosis: ADHD

On Your Experience with Special Needs Before Having Your Child:
JOHN: I was a teacher and administrator for fifteen years. However, I would characterize my experience as broad rather than narrow. I had students in my class with diagnoses but as the general education teacher, it was not my direct responsibility to address this. I was the "content expert," in the classroom. Therefore, I partnered with special education experts and only experienced this area indirectly. I also have

a half-sister who is developmentally delayed. However, I never lived with her and she is 16 years younger than me.

On Your Reaction When You Realized Your Child Was Different?

MARTINA: Denial. I had a surface understanding of ADHD as a teacher, but as a parent it's an ocean of depth. I just wanted to say to the whole situation "no, thanks." But I immediately jumped into reading up on it. I'm a processor and am better at accepting when I gather knowledge on a topic.

JOHN: Obviously, very concerned. I also became defensive of other people's reactions, including my extended family. I was initially resistant to meds but now I am not only accepting, I take them, too. And I felt a lot of empathy for Dale, especially the anxiety that he sometimes feels because I also have ADHD and depression and have an idea of what he is going through.

On Your Feeling at Diagnosis?

JOHN: By the time it came, it was actually a relief. There was a reason why things were happening the way they were and there was a path to follow to help Dale.

On Who in Your World Is on Board with Your Situation and Who Just Can't Give You the Needed Support and Understanding:

JOHN: Martina's Mom has always been Dale's champion. Her dad and my parents just kind of don't get it.

On What Has Gotten Harder Over Time:
JOHN: Anxiety, both for Dale and for us. Sometimes reacting to the reactions of others. Also, his inability to play sports is tough on me. I want him to have what I had socially when I was his age but it doesn't really work.

On What Has Gotten Easier Over Time:
MARTINA: Medication helps with EVERYTHING, whether we are out shopping or if Dale is at school. Once I was able to understand that I was more reacting to being judged by others instead of the behavior, it got easier. Also, letting things go is getting easier.

On How You Find Respite When You Need It:
MARTINA: Work. Bedtime, if I can stay awake past it. My Mom. Travel and weekend getaways. These things have gotten a lot easier as Dale has gotten older.

Do You Think Self-Care Is Important As a Special Needs Parent or Caregiver?
MARTINA: Yes. Because you can't drive on an empty tank.

PRESSURE

For the last couple of years, whenever I would talk to a certain friend of mine, he would remind me, constantly, "You are the glue that holds everything together." He meant it as a compliment, I think. But what it amounted to was that every time he said it, I would feel pressure bearing down on me. It felt like I could never get sick. I could never die. Because what on Earth would happen to my son?

That is a heavy burden to bear. It's as if your right to be human, with a lifespan that will eventually come to an end, has been removed. Yet, at some point, you WILL get sick. You WILL die. And now you have been gifted with an incredible child who may need you for their entire life in a completely different way than a typical child. When you come to this realization, it can be absolutely shocking.

Look, there are some things you can control and some

things you just can't. When you are ready, put some plans in place and share what those plans are with those around you. Ask for help. Both short-term and long-term help. TRAIN those around you to help care for your child with you. TELL them it would be a huge relief if they were aware of how to care for your child's daily needs, just in case of an emergency. And, if you don't have anyone to help, reach out to the schools, the medical people, the therapists, your place of worship, your water polo team, anyone and everyone, and ask them for guidance on how to create this kind of community. Having a back-up person (or, preferably, a team) lifts the heavy ache in your chest. Also, we caregivers tend to be type A people when it comes to our children; we don't want to let go of control. We want our child's care to be done right.

Take the opportunity when you are healthy and well to create this environment for yourself and your child. Relieve the pressure before it becomes unbearable instead of scrambling to do it after you feel like a ton of bricks have fallen on you. You'll be glad you did. Because the fact is, you ARE going to die one day. Who will care for your child? How will this be paid for?

It's already time to plan.

DESIGNATE who will care for your child in the event that something happens to you (ask the person and get their agreement first!). LEGALLY DOCUMENT this. Look into savings plans designed especially for special needs children (yup, that's a thing). Consult with a special needs lawyer (also a thing). DOCUMENT what is required for your child's daily, weekly, monthly, and yearly care. You may not know what all of your child's needs are yet – that's OK. Just document what you know. Document what the diagnoses are, who the doctors are, what the medication is. Create a random list of "Things to Know." Save all of this in a computer file and e-mail it to close family members and friends. But also, PRINT IT OUT and keep it in an obvious place in your home. If something happens to you, your child will be taken care of. And THAT, my fellow caregiver, is worth its weight in gold when it comes to pressure relief.

CHECKING YOUR STRESS AT THE BAGGAGE CHECK

I sometimes have trouble managing my stress. In addition to being a special needs Mom, I have a husband recovering slowly from a long-term illness. Our family is on a fixed income. I have fibromyalgia. I also have anxiety disorder. If you are not familiar with anxiety disorder, it is not the same as plain anxiety. Anxiety means that you have a typical response to a normal situation that makes you anxious. Anxiety disorder means that you have an anxiety response for seemingly no reason. Or an unrealistic reason. So that fight or flight panic experience can pop up when there is no reasonable outside source to trigger it. I am almost always somewhere between tired and exhausted.

Still, I manage. I use techniques to manage my stress. I exercise. I take vitamins. I try to eat healthy. I give myself time-outs to take a break. I practice different forms of self-care. And a lot of the time these things work.

Until they don't.

Recently I have been struggling more than usual. Especially at night. The kids will finally be in bed, asleep. My husband will have finally fallen asleep, too, after I rub his back for a while as I read. And then I lay there, often having a fight or flight response in my body. My breath feels short. My heart feels a bit accelerated. My fingers and toes tingle.

It hurts.

When all else fails and the essential oils don't work (sometimes they do) or having a snack doesn't make it go away (sometimes it does) or distraction with reading or crochet also fails (it often does), then I just have to live with it. I used to drink a small amount of alcohol and it used to numb it. I have practically no tolerance for alcohol so a couple of sips was really all it took. But I have been moving away from that, trying to find a better way.

I created a visualization that has been helping.

You may think this is weird. I kinda think it's weird, too. But sometimes you get to a point where you are willing to try a little weirdness to get some relief. So here it is: It's free, easy to do and you can do it anywhere.

Imagine you are at an empty airport. No one is around and it is quiet and calm. You have a suitcase. It is open and empty. It is ready to be packed. You are going to pack it with your stress, your physical discomfort and your worries.

Take a deep breath. When you breathe out, imagine that whatever is bothering you is being exhaled out of your body and into the suitcase. It can just flow in there or you can exhale it into a nice, folded package and then it can go into the suitcase. Breathe in deeply again. Exhale, and pack some more. Do this several times.

When I do this, sometimes I have stress that feels like it is sitting on my chest. Often, after several repetitions, the physical discomfort eases. My body calms.

Breathe deeply. Exhale it out. Let it flow into the suitcase.

Once I have done this to the point where my body feels more relaxed, I don't want the stress back. So I close the suitcase. I bring it to the baggage check counter. And I check the suitcase.

I'll vary how I do this. Sometimes no one is there and I just put the suitcase on the conveyor belt and watch it get carried away through the hole in the back wall. Sometimes someone is there to take it from me but they are silent and have no discernible characteristics.

You know how people sometimes say "let it go and give it to God?" If God is your jam, you could imagine God standing there, waiting to take your suitcase and check it. If not, no worries. It could be whatever you want it to be.

I created this because I was running out of options and my body and soul were hurting from carrying everything around all the time. I recalled a time when I was hugely pregnant with my daughter, Amaya. I remember jokingly saying to my husband that I loved being pregnant but I wished that, for just 20 minutes, I could put the baby down – she was so heavy! I wanted to put my stress down. Just for a little while.

It worked for me.

Struggling with stress and/or anxiety? Give it try. Can't hurt, might help.

FOLLOW YOUR GUT

Experts become experts through education, training and experience. Because everyone is different, comes from different backgrounds and has different lifestyles, every individual brings something unique to a situation. Additionally, there are different types of education, training and experiences to be had.

This is wonderful. Variety is the spice of life, right?

Until you need an answer to a problem. A plan to proceed. A strategy to implement. And you have no idea what's best.

I grew up with a vision that the world was way more structured than it actually is. Didn't you think that doctors knew everything when you were a kid? That adults had everything under control? It wasn't until I became an adult and experienced a variety of medical situations that I realized treatment plans, protocols and medications aren't nearly as established as the universe would have you believe. I cared for my mom through her breast cancer – lumpectomy, chemo and radiation. And later, my husband and I cared for my mom through a brutal couple of years of Alzheimer's disease. Simultaneously, our son, Kai, who is currently seven and has eight different diagnoses, received his first special needs diagnosis at 18 months.

I have encountered general practitioners, pediatricians, neurologists (including at the Cleveland Clinic), psychologists, social workers, cancer specialists, homeopathic practitioners, essential oil purveyors, physical therapists, occupational therapists, speech and feeding therapists, doctoral candidates, orthopedic therapists, surgeons, MRI specialists, EEG specialists and more. Some of them were phenomenal and some of them sucked dog. As in any profession.

The problem is that when you are trying to take care of the one you love most in the world, your child with special needs, the stakes are high and you want to do what's right. Couple that with perhaps less knowledge of the problem at hand than you would like to have (even if you have studied it in Wikipedia like you were trying to earn a doctorate) and it can be nerve wracking.

What if you make the wrong decision for your child?

The type of professional you choose to guide you in your journey and/or the professional who will provide medication or services to your child can be determined by different things: what type of professional is recommended; who is covered by insurance; word of mouth. Based on the situation, these are usually the top ways one gets in contact. But here is something to keep in mind.

One thought process that may seem obvious but can be overlooked is the fact that the type of practitioner you choose will affect the treatment rendered. In other words, if you approach a psychiatrist for treatment you are most likely to be treated with medication because this is what THEY do. Conversely, if you approach a psychologist for treatment, while they may work with a psychiatrist to get you medication if you need it, the psychologist will probably treat you with therapy, because this is what THEY generally do. Homeopathic and oil people will tend to treat you along a more natural route, i.e. if you have cancer, they will suggest diet changes, supplements, meditation and more. A standard medical doctor will possibly treat the same cancer with surgery, chemo and/or radiation. ABA therapists will use applied behavior analysis for a special needs child, while public school special education classrooms may use that but could just as easily use more traditional modified educational techniques. And these things could be happening in the same building, right next door to each other, as each teacher applies what THEY do (this is not to say that it is not individualized based on the child's needs).

What I want you to take from this is that there is a wide

variety of ways to approach the many issues you're going to face. The only one who is going to be able to make the best guess for which way your child is going to react to a lot of it is YOU. This can feel like a huge weight on your shoulders, especially in areas where medical decisions can mean life or death. Even if the situation is not so severe, it can be a heavy load to carry, to *know* what is going to be the best possible outcome for your child.

So, the next thing to consider is what YOU do. What are your and your family's preferences when it comes to treatment? Are you pro-western medicine with all of the incredible strides it has made historically in solving medical issues? Or does the possibility of side effects, causing someone to grow a third limb while suffering through extreme thirst and dizziness from a new medication, make you want to run screaming for the hills? Do you believe strongly in the power of essential oils? Or are you going to gag if you get one more whiff of lavender oil? Unless it is a life or death situation (and, let's face it, MOST situations are NOT life or death), your choices can be reversed. You can start down a path and then decide that it's not for you and your child. And then try something else. Trial and error doesn't mean that you have necessarily made mistakes. It can also mean that you have successfully figured out what is not going to work for you. It can help you narrow down the playing field.

My son, Kai, who is seven years old, has PVL

(periventricular leukomalacia), which is damaged white brain matter. It is more complicated than that but for the purpose of what we are discussing, that is the information you need to know. He also has several other diagnoses. However, we know that PVL is linked to seizures. This past spring, when he had his first seizure, and the emergency room doctor thought it was related to a high spiking fever, we were hopeful that this was the case, but knew that it could also be from the PVL. The second time he had a seizure, a couple of months later, the emergency room doctor decided it was due to fever and ear infection. I thought that maybe my husband and I knew better. When they wanted to give our son a lumbar puncture, I declined. I wanted to go see a neurologist and get him an EEG to look for seizure activity. Why put our son through a possibly painful test when that probably wasn't it (he had no meningitis symptoms)? PVL is an obscure diagnosis, one that most people (even doctors) are not familiar with. In this case, my husband and I are the experts. And in my gut, I felt that it was related to the PVL. Did I know I was right? No. But all I could do was make the best decision I could with the information I had at the time. And that is all you can do, too.

We went to the neurologist because that is who you need to see to get an EEG. The thing to know about an EEG is that it can only test for seizure activity in the brain DURING the test. So, if you have no seizure activity DURING the test, the test shows no seizure activity. But this does not mean that the patient doesn't get seizures, it just means they didn't during the test. So Kai's EEG came back "normal." Does this mean that he doesn't and will not get seizures? No. So, now what?

The neurologist, who I thought was excellent and liked very much, thought a good plan was to put Kai on an anti-seizure medication for two years. The goal of using the medication is to prevent seizures from occurring during this time and, also, to prevent or reduce seizures for the rest of his life. The medication is also able to assist in developmental delays because it would help Kai to focus and slow down stimming. Sounds dreamy, right?

I am NOT anti-medication. However, as Kai's advocates, it is my husband's and my duty to do our due diligence. This means investigate the medication, read up on its history and possible side effects, and decide whether it would be the best move for Kai.

In this case, the medication that the neurologist was recommending was Trileptal. So we looked it up. It has been used in the United States since 2000 and in Europe since the 1990s. Side effects can include dehydration, nausea, dizziness, a bad rash and more. Additionally, it is possible that if we somehow missed a dose, that event could cause a seizure that WILL NOT STOP.

We chose NOT to use this medication at the time. Why? Kai is nonverbal. Unlike other patients who can communicate, if Kai is having side effect issues, he cannot communicate his discomfort. It becomes a guessing game while he cries or fusses. This can go on for DAYS while we guess at what the problem can be. Also, Kai has sensitive skin and already suffers from eczema. The medication information states that if the rash occurs, we are not to give Kai the next dose before contacting the doctor. What if this happens on a weekend? Missing a dose could cause a seizure that WILL NOT STOP. And, finally, we do not feel that this is an emergency situation. Kai had two mild seizures, a couple of months apart.

So, what are we doing instead? We are trying CBD oil. This is said to control seizures and has a host of other benefits. Kai has been on it for several days and, so far, is doing great on it. I tried it, too. After two days on it, I had to stop because it was making me feel sick. Everyone is different. For Kai, he seems comfortable on it. We will continue with this experiment until the end of the calendar year (four more months) and then revisit the issue. If no seizures, we will continue. If it's not working, we may try the medication. FOLLOW-UP NOTE – it is now nine months later than this original writing. Kai HAS NOT HAD A SEIZURE since he went on CBD oil. He continues to take it and is doing well on it. No side effects. AND he's talking more! Yay!

I will tell you right now that everyone will have an opinion on this. Some will say we are crazy for considering CBD oil. Some will say we are crazy for not following the neurologist's advice, since he works at a top children's hospital in the country, so he obviously must know something. Let me just say this – no one else will be there at 3 AM if Kai has another seizure except me and my husband. No one else will handle the daily living, the events and the aftermath. It is OUR CALL. PERIOD. We are grateful for input and we choose to consult with experts in their fields when we feel the need for information. But we are the executive officers of this corporation. And we decide. Because THERE IS NO ONE IN THE WORLD WHO IS AN EXPERT ON OUR SON EXCEPT US.

YOU are the expert on your child. When you need to make decisions about care there are a few simple steps you can follow to guide you.

Step 1 – Identify the issue.

Step 2 – Decide if it is an emergency. If it is, make the best decision you can based on the information you have at the time and just GO WITH IT. Because that is all you can do. If it is not an emergency, move to the next step.

Step 3 – If it is not an emergency, find out what experts recommend to solve the issue at hand. Remember YOU are the one who decides how to handle the issue. The experts may sometimes give the impression their way is the only way.

Step 4 – Do your due diligence. Read up on the problem and possible solutions. Read about any medicines or therapy methods offered up to you by the experts.

Step 5 – GO WITH YOUR GUT FEELING. If it doesn't feel right, keep researching. Don't be afraid to ask questions. If you find an expert who doesn't want to take the time to answer your questions or makes you feel stupid for asking them, fire that expert and find another. You have the right to ask and they have an obligation to answer in a way you can understand.

Step 6 – Attempt to solve the problem. If it doesn't work, you have successfully found one way that doesn't work and can rule out that method. Then, try another way.

FOLLOW-UP TO FOLLOW YOUR GUT

I had to add this because it is a perfect example of what I was just talking about. It is not about my son, Kai. Instead, it is about my daughter, neurotypical Amaya.

In January 2020, Amaya's entire body broke out in a rash. I didn't know what it was, thought maybe it was chicken pox, and rushed her to our wonderful nurse practitioner. It wasn't chicken pox. It was a really bad outbreak of psoriasis.

There had been signs that something was off. Amaya had had a bad case of scalp dandruff that had started to scale over. I had no idea why that was happening. I kept trying to treat it with dandruff products and when those didn't work, I took her to the pharmacist and showed him her scalp, saying, "What's that?" (If you have never done this before, pharmacists are highly knowledgeable and can often save you a trip to the doctor for something like this. He thought maybe it was a fungal infection so we tried those products. This time he was wrong. But he's often right!).

We attempted to get an appointment with a dermatologist and had to wait a month. Then we drove an hour and a half to the appointment (remember, we live in the woods in East Texas). I hated the clinic. They took a biopsy and yes, Bob, it was psoriasis. They gave us topical meds and sent us on our way with another follow-up appointment in a couple of weeks. The topical meds didn't work. Then we were referred to Dallas Children's hospital (the same building where we saw Kai's neurologist, who was pissed off because we didn't choose his prescription and gave Kai the CBD oil instead). This was the beginning of the pandemic of 2020. While there were multiple medication options to get Amaya's psoriasis under control, all of them SUPPRESSED THE IMMUNE SYSTEM.

So, I'm sitting in the examination room with Amaya and the pediatrician tells me there are about 25 different medications Amaya can take and various ways to administer the meds. My husband was home with Kai so I was the only parent present. WHAT DID I WANT TO DO?

ARE YOU KIDDING ME? How was I to know? If her immune system was suppressed, and she was at school (schools hadn't closed yet) could she get really sick? I felt that familiar deer-in-the-headlights feeling. What if I made the wrong choice?

Thank goodness I had prepared myself by following

the steps above. It applied, even though this was my neurotypical child, not my child with special needs. I had IDENTIFIED THE ISSUE (finally). I had realized this was not an emergency situation (although, unknown to me, the pandemic was coming and compromising her immune system wasn't something I might have done if I had known the severity of what was approaching). SO I ASKED THE EXPERT (the doc) WHAT THEY THOUGHT I SHOULD DO. And, ever so helpfully, she told me that the choice was up to me (thanks, Doc). So I asked what she would do if it were her child? Again, no preferential answer. You never know what you're going to get with the docs, huh? The neurologist was POSITIVE his meds were for Kai and Amaya's doc completely deferred the choice to me. Sigh. Can we find a positive middle ground? But that's another topic. Thank goodness, I had done my DUE DILIGENCE. I had read up on psoriasis and the possible medication paths we could take. I knew the possible side effects. I knew the pros and cons. This was also helpful when the doc ran through all of this information during our meeting – it wasn't the first time I was hearing it. I had had an opportunity to reflect and let it soak in.

I asked Amaya what her preferences were (Needles or pills? Medicine every day, every week or every season? Light therapy?). Then I asked the doctor about research. What was the medicine that had been around the longest? What was the medicine they had the most data on? What was the medicine she prescribed that appeared to have the best results? Then I MADE THE DECISION WITH THE INFORMATION I HAD AT THAT TIME AND IN THAT PLACE. I chose a medicine that had been around the longest with a good track record, which had shown the least side effects. I also liked that they would continually monitor Amaya in case her body was having any functional issues and that we could go off the medicine at any time without penalty (unlike with that seizure medicine they had wanted to give Kai, remember? The one that could have triggered a seizure that wouldn't stop?).

Amaya has been on the meds for a couple of months now. She went from having psoriasis on 90% of her body to about 10%. We are still in process and things are looking good. I'm nervous because of the pandemic, that we have lowered her body's immune system in order to fight this. So I am extra vigilant that we and Amaya socially distance ourselves and follow the current medical procedures and recommendations.

This was the best decision I could make at the time, given what was presented. It was all I could do. That's all you can do, too. If you follow the steps, you can make the decisions necessary to the best of your ability. Will the choices be perfect? Nothing ever is. But sometimes they have to be made and this will help you do the best you can.

You can do this.

CRAFTING YOUR SPECIAL NEEDS LIFE WHEN EVERYONE HAS AN OPINION

When you have a baby, EVERYONE has an opinion on how you should handle them. And they TELL YOU, often whether you want to hear their opinion or not.

They tell you not to let the baby sleep on the stomach. They tell you not to let the baby sleep on the back. The zealous breastfeeding patrol comes after you with a vengeance – because if you don't breastfeed you will NEVER have a strong bond (I am two generations into proving this one wrong). You should add an extra layer of clothing when outdoors. Wait – take that extra layer away, the baby will be too hot!

And then they start telling you what you should be doing as a new parent, for yourself.

Go out on a date night, they say. It'll strengthen your marriage, having had a new baby. Never mind that if you don't sleep soon you will pass out – you should dress up, go out and RECONNECT with your partner, right now. BUT don't leave the baby too soon. They will have separation anxiety. Anxious? Have a glass of wine, it will calm you down. But not if you breastfeed!!!

With all of the advice flying around when having a typical child, the pressure to do it "right," especially with the first baby, can be tremendous. I remember absolutely bawling because my new baby daughter and I could not get breastfeeding to work. The breastfeeding patrol (all right, the nursing staff and breastfeeding specialists but man, are these folks CONVINCED it's the way to go) worked with us endlessly but the milk just wasn't coming in and she was starting to actually lose weight in her first 48 hours. I finally switched her to formula and everything worked out just fine. Some people say the bond is not the same but we could not be closer as mother and daughter (same thing happened with me and my mother, by the way). But I wish someone would have eased my stress by saying it's not a failure if you can't make breastfeeding work. That formula is OK, too. But no one did.

Moving on in time, I was more than blessed to have a son with special needs. He is now seven years old. And let me tell you, if you want to quiet all of the advice-giving and background noise that occurs when you have a typical child, have a child with special needs. Want to really confuse them? Have a child with eight different diagnoses.

For the longest time, all I heard were the proverbial crickets chirping. NO ONE HAD A CLUE.

And then the barrage of advice continued, albeit a bit differently.

Instead of sounding confident that their advice was the right thing, their presentation became wary.

"I don't know if this would work since your child is different, but for my child, this [INSERT ADVICE HERE] worked really well!"

Here's where both situations have something important in common. They are background noise in the life you are creating for yourself. This is NOT to say advice can't be valuable or useful. But especially when living the special needs life, it is extremely important you CRAFT your life in a way that works for you, your child and your family. People don't talk about this. CRAFTING your life seems foreign. A whole lot of people live life letting it happen to them. Here's where you can make a difference for yourself.

What kind of life do you want to have? What kind of daily life will make it easier for YOUR particular family situation to not only survive but thrive? Typical families have it far easier in a lot of ways but families with special needs MUST consider this question carefully.

Do you feel like your daily situation is working for you? Or do you wish your fairy godmother would come in and overhaul everything with a wave of her magic wand?

Or – here's one a lot of parents can relate to – is there

a part of your day you just dread because EVERY SINGLE DAY it goes wrong and you just can't bear it anymore? As in, morning is OK, coffee is working, activities go by, everything is fine but you are just DREADING whatever o'clock because almost every single day something happens to set your child with special needs off and you can't bear the thought of it?

How did I know this about you? Well, let's just say I've been there.

Here's where CRAFTING your life comes in.

While the well-wishers mean well and the do-gooders are trying to do good, they don't really understand, do they? They haven't walked your walk.

Do yourself a favor. Smile and nod. Tell them you are SO APPRECIATIVE of their words of wisdom and will definitely take their input into consideration. SMILE. And never think about their input again if you don't find it valuable.

It is FRUSTRATING when they seem like they know it all about YOUR special needs life, isn't it? They truly don't know. And you have bigger fish to fry than to waste a single second being annoyed at them.

Instead, take the time you would have spent being annoyed and think about this – if you have a specific situation or time period of your day that is JUST NOT WORKING, what can you do to CRAFT it differently? Instead of it happening to you every day, what if you made choices that created a different outcome?

Sometimes this seems impossible. Insurmountable.

It's not.

I know you are exhausted, so creative problem solving isn't necessarily your strong suit right now. But you need to do SOMETHING to craft your life because it isn't going to craft itself. Try this:

1) Focus on a small piece of your day. Maybe it is the waking up process. Maybe it's the lunch making process if you make lunch for your child to take to school (picky eaters, aren't they?). Maybe it's bath time.

2) Isolate the problem. Is it that the mornings are rushed and rushing makes your child with special needs crazy? Make lunch, lay out clothes, and bathe the night before. Putting shoes on to go to the bus becomes a battle every single day? Let it go, at least for a while. Maybe the two of you can pick out special character "walking to the bus" slippers and send shoes to school in the backpack. How amazing would it be if being creative and a little flexible ends a months-long streak of daily meltdowns? The key is to MAKE A PLAN. One that works FOR YOU AND YOUR CHILD. Not necessarily what the people in your life whispering in your ear think would work for THEIR child. They may not agree with how you are going to handle things. They don't have to. It's YOUR world.

3) Execute the plan. Try it out for a couple of days.

4) Evaluate. How did it go? Is it working? Is your stress

easing for that particular time of the day? If yes, keep going! If not, try something new. Keep trying something new until it works.

Then, you take this system and apply it to another part of your day. And another. Until soon, you have CRAFTED your life. It applies to every area, too, not just to raising a child with special needs. Of course, there are things you will have no control over, things you can't craft. But there are SO MANY things you CAN craft. Try it. You'll see.

"They" are going to tell you what they think about what you are doing. Because EVERYBODY has an opinion.

Everybody does have an opinion. But not everybody's opinion matters.

Whose opinion matters? Yours. Is it working for you and your child? Yes? BOOM!!!!

That's all that matters.

You've got this.

Originally published on the blog, livingthespecialneedslife.com on 4/30/19

AVOID BURNOUT
DON'T BE A SHOOTING STAR

Imagine a shooting star. It is bright and stands out amongst the other stars in the sky. It dazzles. Imagine you are watching it shoot across the sky, past all the other stars. Your eyes are drawn to it. It is thrilling. It is the most amazing, best one.

Then it is gone.

And what is left? The stars that are stationary. They are less bright, but still shining. They persist. And they are also beautiful. The shooting star is but a memory while the remaining stars shine.

Now imagine this. You are running a marathon. But you are running it as fast as you possibly can from the first steps you take. You are in a full sprint. You have to go 26.2 miles as fast as you possibly can. How likely is it that you will complete the marathon, going full speed, without burning out?

The sprinter and the shooting star both have something in common. They are operating at full capacity. Quickly, their time of excellence is over.

If you give 110% of yourself to ANYTHING, you will soon purge yourself of the energy you need to conserve to continue. This description of high devotion sounds impressive and committed, doesn't it? But because it is impossible to maintain due to limits in energy, time, and resources, it can only be achieved for a brief period of time, if at all.

This is something we, as special needs caregivers, cannot afford.

While we want to do "our best" for our amazing angels, defining what our best is and measuring it against what other people appear to have in terms of energy and best effort is also a fruitless comparison. They are not you and you are not them.

So how do you set the pace when living the special needs life?

The first step is to set an amount of goals that are manageable for you and your child. For example, my son, who is six years old and has special needs, has a lot of different things to work on. His hands are not strong (and he is highly unmotivated in this area), so he needs to work with puzzles. And playdough. And a peg board. And writing. And coloring. And lacing (which we haven't even started). He needs to practice zipping, buttoning, cutting and any other kind of object manipulation. But he also needs help with speech. And gross motor activities. And feeding (although we may just end up eating purees, AKA baby food, for a long, long time and that's OK).

I'm sure I am leaving things out but this is a good start on our list of things to work on. Imagine what would happen if I gave 110% all of the time to ALL of this. Or even to six of these things. Having made this mistake in the past, I can tell you the outcome isn't pretty. You only have a certain amount of time in an hour, a day, a week, a lifetime. You can work on anything you want. But you can't work on EVERYTHING, or even most things, at the same time, going full speed, 110%. The more goals you work on, the less effective this strategy becomes.

This is also true as a caregiver and as a human. In your own life, the thinner you spread yourself, the less energy you can put into each thing you are working on. This is not to say you can't do many things at the same time and do them well. We are, after all, a society of multitaskers. But you can't give 110% all the time to everything without the inevitable burnout.

The second step, after you have identified which goals you are going to work on, and shortened the list to what is truly manageable and meaningful for right now, is to set the pace. You want to shine like a star but not burn out like a shooting star. So what percentage of your time, energy and resources can you give, continuously, to your goals, which is sustainable over time? That amount is different for everyone. Sometimes "good enough" is going to have to take the place of "perfect."

Teaching is an excellent example of this. When I was a teacher in the classroom, I really had to learn to set long- and short-term goals, pace myself and realize that the list of what needed to be accomplished got longer, every single day. You could work 24 HOURS A DAY and NEVER accomplish it all. I had to set the pace for myself so things could get done and, most importantly, I would have the energy to come back tomorrow. Since my most important goal was the excellence of my students, sometimes the bulletin boards I had to decorate in the hallways had to be "good enough." Cute, but nothing special. I was not one of "those" teachers, who could turn every art project into a masterpiece with ease. I'm so jealous of them (I mean, aren't you?).

I realized if I wanted to shine when teaching, I could work at 75-85% of what I felt was my capacity of time, energy and focus and still come back the next day. Most importantly, I could do this CONSISTENTLY.

I cannot, however, do this with my son at home as consistently. Sometimes I drop the ball. Sometimes we skip working on something we "should" work on (do you "should" on yourself, too?). Because I am human. But I try to work with him at about 70-80% of my capacity most of the time. If you haven't noticed yet, these percentages are unofficial. I do it by feel.

The third step is to check in with yourself daily. How are you feeling? Are you tired, stressed, overwhelmed? Did your child sleep through the night for the first time in weeks and you got some rest? Adjust your efforts to your goals that day accordingly.

The fourth step is to reevaluate your goals for your child over time. It is NOT a failure if something either isn't working or isn't going as quickly as you anticipated. It is smart to examine what is working and what is not. Maybe you need to come back to reading a book to your child when you are on the fourth day in a row of complete rebellion. Instead of ramping up your energy in this area, back off. Focus somewhere else. And come back to it at a later time. If you are functioning at 75-85% of your capacity, why waste it in an area that is not working right now?

The fifth step is to leave yourself room to WOW. You know how sometimes you want to pull out all of the stops on something and go at that full 110%? For yourself, for your child? If you leave yourself room in your energy level, time, and resources, you CAN be a shooting star. You CAN sprint. Just not all of the time. Pull out that last bit of reserved energy, time, and effort every now and then to really shine. Bake the eight-layer cake your child loves. Work on shoe tying relentlessly for a week (if your child doesn't rebel). Make a deadline at your job and have the best bulletin board at the school where you teach (this is SO

EXTRA, what's my deal?).

The sixth and last step is to recharge. You can't function at any level, long term, without taking breaks and taking proper care of yourself. If you, like so many other special needs caregivers, have dropped the ball in this area, that's OK. But do yourself a favor and pick the ball up. NOW. Today. Self-care, while a buzz-word in our society, is an absolute must when living the special needs life. Take a break. Sit on your porch swing and have a cup of something steaming hot (or ice cold). And pat yourself on the back. You are doing it!

Just a quick reminder about self-care. If you decide you need to exercise to take care of yourself, remember that this is a LIFELONG practice. Don't go 110% the first day! You won't be able to walk and won't want to come back tomorrow.

Living the special needs life (or any life) is a marathon. You are going the distance, not going for speed (I think I just quoted Cake – the band, not the dessert). You can do and have and be almost anything but you can't do and have and be everything, all at the same time, and do it well.

Do it well. For yourself. For your child.

Originally published on the blog, livingthespecialneedslife.com on 2/17/19

CHANGING YOUR INNER DIALOGUE FOR SUCCESS AND PEACE WHEN LIVING THE SPECIAL NEEDS LIFE

There is no one I have ever met who is as mean to me as I sometimes am to myself, and I don't do it that often, but when I do, it is surprisingly harsh. I just started being mean to myself a few years ago, right around the time my mother passed away after a harsh battle with Alzheimer's disease. My son had been diagnosed with disabilities at the same time and we had a hard couple of years.

My mother was gone. Things were still nuts. I was still working full time, our son was having up to ten therapy sessions a week and we were trying to sell our house in Las Vegas to move back to Texas. We had never wanted to leave Texas in the first place but since my mother refused to move and she needed help, we had joined her in Las Vegas.

I was mourning HARD. My mother was my best friend, my champion. There was no one who had loved me as she had. I felt empty. I was going through her things, getting rid of stuff. I had never realized she was such a packrat. She saved every paper, every receipt. She had the heating bill from the house I grew up in, which she had moved out of twenty years prior. It was a lot and it was difficult.

One night, I was sitting quietly by myself and I thought "I miss my mother." What followed in my brain was a barrage of nastiness.

My brain said, "Well, tough. You will never, ever see her again. She's never coming back. She's gone. Never, ever, never, ever. Too bad. You will have to live like this. You will never feel better again. You will never feel happy again. And you helped her to die so it's your fault." I had honored my mother's wishes by bringing her to hospice and having her sedated. She had chosen to stop eating and drinking and told me she wanted to die. She had had a long, hard road and it wasn't going to get any better. I did what she wanted. I was having an extremely difficult time with this.

I felt like someone else was in the room, and they were incredibly mean. Only, for the first time in my life, that someone was me. I was incredibly stressed and I'm sure that played a part in it.

I told no one. And then it started happening, repeatedly. I would be doing whatever daily chore I needed to do and, in my mind, I would think, "I miss my mother." And the insults would start.

It was devastating. It was becoming hard to live with.

On some level, though, it was true. It wasn't my fault, but in this life, she was gone. And in this life, I would never, ever see her again.

I was nowhere near any self-care. I was not seeing a therapist, although, Lord knows, it would have been helpful. I wasn't talking about it with my husband, who was also stressed beyond belief, trying to keep our life together, get the house cleaned up, get it sold and get home, all while participating in ten therapy sessions a week in our home for our son. I didn't want to lay one more thing on him.

One day, when it had happened again and I felt like I had just gotten beaten up, I decided I needed to figure out a solution or I was going to go nuts. I thought hard about it and decided I was going to REPLACE the words my brain was saying to me. The only thing I could think of was the word YES. I missed my mother. YES. All the other words, when they came, were to be immediately cut off and covered with a loud, resounding YES in my brain. If my brain continued to respond, I would just repeat YES. In my thoughts. Loudly. I was going to cut off this mean mental process that had taken me over. This meanie was not going to be allowed to win. After all, how dare this mental person be mean to me after what I had just gone through?

It took a few days to overpower the thoughts. Now, almost five years later, what I put into place is automatic for my brain. Any time the thought filters through my head, "I miss my mother," my brain automatically says in response,

"Yes." There is nothing else to say. I can't do anything about it. This is sufficient. I acknowledge the feeling. YES.

I then started to think about if there were other times when my brain was not as nice to me as I would like. I realized this also happens, sometimes, when I think about my son.

My son has PVL (periventricular leukomalacia), Duplicate Chromosome 16, Autism, SPD, Apraxia and more. We don't know why he has any of these things. Specifically for PVL, which is damaged white brain matter, there is usually a list of things that could have caused it. In our case, none of these reasons were present. We will never know why.

I realized my brain sometimes blames me. It is sometimes not as nice to me as it could be. When these thoughts come, they are HARSH. It is not my fault. Fault doesn't even really matter because an admission of fault changes nothing. And my son is incredible. He is my happy-go-lucky angel, with not a care in the world, doing well in school and thriving.

I applied the same principal to getting my thoughts under control. I REPLACED them with kinder thoughts. I fought back against this stream of thought. Any time my brain began to harass me about this, I would reply, loudly but silently, in my head, "THAT IS NOT ALLOWED." Because my brain, first and foremost, needed to be kind to me.

This doesn't mean everything is rosy and I don't

accept responsibility for things. But I know when excessive meanness is being played out in my thoughts.

You can use this, too. Not every thought that goes through your head is true. Not every thought that goes through your head is appropriate. If your brain starts treating you badly, there is no reason why you have to accept this behavior. If you wouldn't (and you shouldn't!) accept this type of treatment from someone else, you sure as heck shouldn't allow it in your brain either.

When you choose to replace your inner dialog with something supportive and comforting, you create a better life for yourself. This is a technique you can use anytime, anywhere. It's free. And it works. Try it.

Originally published on the blog, livingthespecialneedslife.com on 1/15/19

HOW TO IDENTIFY ASSETS AND LIABILITIES TO MAKE POSITIVE CHANGE WHEN LIVING THE SPECIAL NEEDS LIFE

Two of the things I am much more limited on since becoming a special needs parent are time and patience. I find most of the time I am patient with my 6-year-old son, and I give him most of my time. After him, the rest of my family is next. My 8-year-old, neurotypical daughter, my husband, my older kids and my grandkids take up a lot of my world. I like it this way. But there is not much left after that.

Add in self-care (or at least, I try to add in self-care) and my time and patience dwindle down even more. I just don't have the inclination to spend what's left on people and situations that don't benefit me. I am much more apt to end relationships, leave situations that are not working, replace therapists and modify to-do lists than I ever was.

Sometimes, though, it is hard to identify who and what

should stay in my life and at what level.

When I first met my husband, he introduced me to the concept of thinking of people as assets or liabilities. Later on, I added in thinking of situations in these same terms.

Who and what are worth their weight in gold to you?

An asset is simply someone or something, or perhaps a situation, of value or use to you. A liability? Something or someone who puts you at a disadvantage. Perhaps a situation is more trouble than it's worth.

If you are a special needs parent or caregiver, you probably have less surplus time, patience and energy than ever before. I know I do. It is to your advantage to periodically review people and situations in your life to make sure only the most valuable get your time and attention.

Let's talk about relationships with people. Are the people in your life an asset to you? Do you feel at peace when you spend time with them? Do they enhance your life? Do they energize you? Do you learn from them? Are they living a lifestyle you would like to emulate? Do you admire them? Have they achieved things you would like to achieve? Do they lift your spirits? Does spending time with them bring you joy? Are they supportive? Are they there for you in a crisis? Do they understand, honor and support your living the special needs life, even if they are inexperienced with special needs people? If you can answer yes to at least some of these questions about a person, then this person could be an asset to you.

Are there people in your life who are a liability? When you are with them, do they suck the energy right out of the room for you? Do they put you down? Are they unsupportive when you talk about your hopes and dreams? When you are with them, do you feel on edge? Are they stagnant in their own lives? Do you feel depressed or upset after spending time with them? Are they manipulative? Do they require more emotional energy than you can possibly give? Does spending time with them tend to steal your joy? Do they tend to disappear if you need them? Do they disregard you are living the special needs life in favor of what is important to them? If you can answer yes to at least some of these questions about a person, then this person could be a liability to you.

It is the same with situations. The therapy you are taking your child with special needs to – asset or liability? Is your child making progress? Do you dread going because of the therapist's personality? Does the session end in joy or tears for your child? If you decide the therapy/therapist is more of a liability than an asset, guess what? It's time to give it up and find someone/something else. Having difficulty getting your needs met with the school administration? Go over their heads (yes, you can do that!). The boss has a boss! Deal with someone who can be an asset to you. Your child can't afford for this relationship to be a liability. Adjust accordingly. Doing business with someone who is unprofessional? You can't always leave the arrangement but if it is within your control, take your business to someone who respects your time and delivers the product you deserve to have. If you can't leave it, it is time for a serious talk about your expectations. Be honest and forthcoming and you may turn this liability into an asset.

Once you start identifying the assets and liabilities in your life, it is time to make some adjustments. Where will you put more of your time? Where will you spend less of your time? It is not selfish to spend less time around people who are more of a liability to you than an asset; it is essential to your special needs life. Have relatives you are beginning to recognize as more of a liability than an asset? You may not be able to completely cut them out but you can certainly limit the time spent with them. You may even realize someone you haven't been spending much time with lately is a huge asset to you. Adjust accordingly.

This process of examining your life and crafting it to your needs is eye opening. Sometimes, in the endless whirl of living the special needs life you don't stop to think about the stress others add to your world. Or, conversely, the joy. You have the power to balance your life by adjusting your world – spend more time with your assets and limit or end time with your liabilities.

This is a tremendous act of self-care. You know how people are always telling you to take care of yourself? They tell you to limit your stress by doing a favorite activity, exercising, meditating, anything that is stress relieving. I'm not knocking this – I do it and I need it. However, take it one step further! Embrace the power examining assets and liabilities in your life gives you – an opportunity to not just manage stress, but take some of it away.

Originally published on the blog, livingthespecialneedslife.com on 1/15/19

MOVING FROM STRENGTH, NOT FEAR

I used to be a teacher in a school that was, shall we say, CHALLENGING. It was a Title 1 school, low income, in a neighborhood that often had visits from first responders. Sometimes, at recess, we would hear gun shots. Although the teachers would be alert to checking for the safety of our students, our students had become used to it and often wouldn't respond to the sounds at all. To them, it was just another sound in their daily lives.

Our staff went through a lot. It was an elementary school but our students had already lived through enough that many were old, tired souls. We dealt with drug possession, weapons possession, sexual interactions on campus (at five and six years old), violence, custody battles and more on a daily basis (often more than daily). Our students were often unable to use their imaginations in the classroom. Their daily experiences had taught them this was not a thing of value and they practically had this beaten out of them. Therefore, writing fiction, making art and being creative was extremely hard for them. They had to be practical to survive from a young age.

We learned as teachers to become subversive to get what our students needed. There were rules but there were ways around them if you were persistent. I was quite persistent. My students were not going to go without, not on my watch. I fed them, clothed them, cleaned them up, broke up their fights, separated their sexual interactions with as much grace as possible, loved on them hard and went home exhausted every night to crash out for a few hours before getting up the next day to do it again. I made visits to illegal businesses when I couldn't track the parents down at home. I tried not to inhale too deeply when I did visits at the actual homes. I attended funerals of family members who had been shot. And, after all of this was accomplished, I still had to teach them the curriculum. I was not a one woman show – the staff at this school was an incredible team.

The students had a lot of "special needs." I wouldn't categorize them as the "people with special needs," I usually talk about on the blog, but they did, in fact, need to be handled and cared for in a different way than typical students.

Sometimes I did things that walked the line.

Suffice to say it was for the greater good and taking a

risk for myself to get my students what they needed seemed, at the time, like a trade-off I was willing to make.

I recall one day I was going about the building, trying to gather resources my students needed, when I ended up sidelined by the school counselor. I was absolutely doing something I wasn't supposed to be doing, to get things I wasn't necessarily supposed to be getting, to give things to those who definitely were not supposed to be getting them. My usual mode of operation.

The counselor pulled me aside and told me I shouldn't be doing what I was doing. Yes, the students desperately needed what I was trying to accomplish, but I could GET IN TROUBLE. I looked into this woman's eyes and saw fear there, for herself and for me. She began to list all of the possible things that could go wrong if I made the decisions that needed to be made for the good of my students. I could GET REPRIMANDED. People might DISAGREE WITH MY DECISIONS. My superiors might be UPSET AND DISAPPOINTED with my choices. I might even GET WRITTEN UP.

I calmly waited for her to finish. Then I looked her straight in the eye and said, "If you are going to do this job and you are going to do it the way it needs to be done, you can't move from fear. You HAVE TO MOVE FROM STRENGTH. If I moved from fear, I would never get anything done for these kids. Fear has no place in my decision making process when I am here." And I walked away, leaving her standing there, mouth agape. I had no time for fear.

Did I feel fear? Of course I did. But I wasn't allowing it to rule my decisions or my actions.

Feeling fear is an important ability. When you have a mental or physical response to something, which you categorize as fearful, your body is telling you to be alert to danger. The problem is when you allow it to overcome rational decision making. You need to be able to take the information you have and make the best decision you can make with it at the time. You also need to be able to see the possible outcomes, both positive and negative, while controlling your fear response so you don't get overwhelmed. These are not innate skills you are born with. It is a learning process, which takes time, practice and patience to master.

What does this have to do with living the special needs life? With being a parent or caregiver of a child with special needs? EVERYTHING.

You may have to move mountains to get what your child needs. You will be presented with situations you never dreamed of when deciding you wanted to be a parent. Your child may do things you never imagined having to deal with. And you will sometimes be overwhelmed.

THIS IS A NORMAL RESPONSE.

When you take a look around at all of the other parents who appear to have it all together and seem able to manage everything while you are struggling with even the simple things, I guarantee you at some point you will feel fear. I mean, who wouldn't? Your child is DIFFERENT. Your situation is DIFFERENT. Your way of doing things most definitely will look DIFFERENT (are you sensing a pattern here?).

And being different, doing things differently, having a different situation, isn't easy. When you look around for support from others, they are not always going to understand. They will look with fear at the sometimes outrageous things you do while living the special needs life. They will question your decisions. They will warn you – BE CAREFUL!!! Don't get in trouble! Don't rock the boat!

We who are living the special needs life do not have the luxury of living in fear. We can't. Our children with special needs are depending on us to make some tough choices in a timely manner so we may move on to the next tough choices. And the next ones.

When you get paralyzed with fear, the "oh, crap" feeling of what if this or that happens, your power becomes diminished. You stop moving from strength. And you know who suffers? The ones who are most important. Our children.

Do yourself a favor and stop carrying the fear of the world on your shoulders when you make decisions for yourself and your child. Yes, there are possible repercussions to every decision you make. Make the decisions anyway. Do your best with the information you have at the time. Make the decision and accept the consequences whether they show up now, later, or never.

They say teaching is a subversive activity. That goes double for parenting when living the special needs life. Do what needs to be done, in whatever way you need to do it to make sure the one who needs it the most gets it. Then pat yourself on the back. And come back tomorrow to do it again.

Originally published on the blog, livingthespecialneedslife.com on 3/7/19

NO ONE HAS IT ALL FIGURED OUT

I was a full-time stepmom to three amazing, neurotypical kids before I became a birth mother. When I became their parent, I went from having no kids, to having three kids, full time. However, since the youngest one was already six, they were past diapers, past toilet training, past all of the baby stuff I found absolutely bewildering. It was a big adjustment but I had already been a teacher for several years, so I had some clue of how to care for them.

Not so when my first birth-child, a neurotypical girl, was a newborn. I remember sitting at the local mall food court with the baby and my mother. My son, who is special needs, was not yet born. My baby daughter was a few weeks old. I was struggling. Thankfully, my husband, a veteran father by this point, was able to teach me so much about how to care for a newborn. But he wasn't there that day.

My daughter was sleeping. It was the middle of the day on a weekday so lots of older folks were out and about and several smiled at my baby as they passed by. And I remember talking to my mother about how overwhelmed I was feeling.

Nearby, I observed a mother and FOUR girls sitting at a table. They were obviously sisters, looking alike. They were all perfectly dressed. They were sitting calmly at their table, talking quietly and eating their lunch. The oldest one may have been five though they were all close in age. The mother was perfectly dressed as well, nails done, hair coiffed. I just kept watching them in astonishment. Here I was, with ONE child and my mother to help, and I felt like a wreck. When I lifted my daughter from her car seat/stroller combo, I noticed I had chosen a onesie with a stain on the bottom, which hadn't been obvious to me when I dressed her that morning. This woman had FOUR kids and herself dressed perfectly, and my baby had on a stained onesie.

I remember feeling like this woman I was observing had it all together. And I would NEVER, EVER have it all figured out like she did.

Fast forward several years. This past December, I am sitting in my son's special needs classroom for a holiday party. My son has evolved to a point where his Dad and I can come visit the classroom without it causing a huge meltdown because it disrupts his day. This was a hard-won achievement. He is sitting on a chair with his classmates at circle time, singing along (OK, babbling along) and cuddling my leg. Across the carpet, another mom is struggling. Her son is crying like crazy because there are parents in the room and THAT IS NOT WHAT WE USUALLY DO. The mother is distressed. My heart goes out to her. And I think, if I were her looking up at me, I might appear like I have it all together.

This makes me smile inside because it is so far from being true.

Comparing yourself to other parents, especially other parents of special needs children, is a quick route to insanity.

From a logical perspective, it is simply not possible for the food court mother to have had it all together every single minute of every day. Heck, yeah, she was having a great moment that day in the food court, but can you imagine having four girls that close together in age? Conversely, it is not possible for the mom at the class party to have every single minute of every day with her child be a wreck. You know they must have good moments. That just wasn't one of them.

When you compare your life, of which you know every single detail, with the slice of life you see in other people, of which you know few details, you are comparing apples and oranges. The next time you feel like you are the only one who doesn't have it all figured out, remember NO ONE HAS IT ALL FIGURED OUT. How could they?

You do the best you can at the time. Sometimes your family will look put together and fantastic. You will walk proudly with your child with special needs, head held high. Other times, you and your child will be a mess.

Let's refocus. Instead of worrying about how you appear to others or trying to appear LIKE others, keep your eye on the prize. Your child is the prize. If a meltdown ensues, even in public, caring for them is priority number one. If someone sees you on your best day, well, they lucked out, didn't they? And if someone sees your slice of life on your worst day, well what they think about it is their business, not yours.

Worrying about having it all figured out is a burden you can put down right now. You will NEVER have it all figured out. And that's OK.

Originally published on the blog, livingthespecialneedslife.com on 1/31/19

POST-TRAUMATIC GROWTH WHEN LIVING THE SPECIAL NEEDS LIFE – IT'S A THING

I think when I was younger, I had a vision of me being who I was throughout the rest of my life. I mean, I knew I would change over time but I never thought there would be life events that broke who I was into before and after.

There have been several events that have done this. Getting married was a life event, and certainly warrants a before and after, but I didn't feel my personality changed drastically. What really changed me were three different, specific events. One was the diagnosis of Alzheimer's disease and, after two years of caring for her, the subsequent suicide of my mother. Another was my son being diagnosed with a myriad of special needs. And the third one was having a sick husband. In fact, as I type this, I am sitting in a hospital cafeteria, awaiting tests results for him, to find out if he has had a major relapse. He has been doing so much better since last year, but some tests came back that were a cause for concern. So here we are at the hospital. Again.

Having had these three events come in a span of only a couple of years brought me to a dark, black and white, joyless place. I felt like I was never going to be happy again. How could I? I lost my mother, my best friend, to a vicious disease where, by the end, she didn't even know who I was. My son was never going to be "normal" (I had no idea of the joys of raising a son with special needs yet, it was quite the gift in disguise). And my husband almost died.

Bleak indeed.

I stopped taking care of myself. My needs, wants, joys, desires, pleasures, were the last thing I had time to focus on. It seemed selfish to think "what about me?" So, I didn't. And that backfired in a big way.

Self-care when you are a caregiver is counter intuitive. My intuition was always to put those I love, who are struggling, first. It made perfect sense to me. The ones who needed the most care, got it. And I, well, I wasn't sick, I didn't have a diagnosis that needed addressing, so I was last.

The problem with this was there is only so much energy and effort one can give without replenishing the source. I didn't know this, then, not really. I mean, I knew it intellectually. But I'm stubborn. So, I was JUST FINE. Until I wasn't.

I functioned on empty for a long time and it felt really bad.

After my mom died, after my son got into therapy, after my husband mostly recovered, after we moved to be closer to family for help when we needed it, I finally had time to take a breath. I didn't like how I felt. I didn't like what I saw in the mirror. I didn't laugh anymore. I seemed incapable of having fun. And I was stuck like this for a long time.

I am finally, in this past twelve months, coming out of it. I invested some serious time into some serious self-care. I began to walk daily, at first only fifteen minutes but now I have worked up to 80 minutes most days. I forced myself to read jokes on the internet to make me smile. I started projects I had long ago put down. I completely cut out alcohol (although I have next to no tolerance anyway, so we are talking about maybe 2 ounces a day, which is a lot for me). I tried to schedule things into my day that brought me joy. I added in a small amount of yoga every day as well, and started listening to music again. I didn't do this all at the same time. It was gradual, a progression.

I have just met the new me. And I am liking who I've met.

I recently came across a concept called post-traumatic growth. When I started reading about it, it resonated with me immediately. It describes what happens when a terrible, harsh event occurs in your life that triggers growth afterwards for you. This is exactly what happened to me, although it took several years for the growth to occur.

I like myself so much better now than I did before. I'm

not sure how I feel about that.

I am not happy that any of these events occurred (this is even more complex with feelings about my son, whom I adore just the way he is, but you get it, right?). But I am happy with how the changes have affected me in the end. And the changes couldn't have happened without these events. So, my growth is a positive thing that came out of a series of negative, difficult, emotionally draining events.

How weird is that?

Apparently, not so weird. I've read that post-traumatic growth is apparently more common than post-traumatic stress disorder (PTSD).

I am certainly not suggesting my trauma is anything close to what military folk experience in battle, like I read about. But as my mother always said, just because the person next to you has two broken legs doesn't mean your one broken leg doesn't hurt. My experiences were traumatic, for me.

This doesn't mean a traumatic event is a positive thing. It isn't. But people are reporting in large numbers they are experiencing growth after traumatic events. For me, a myriad of things have changed and instilled growth in me, including:

-I have redefined what it means to be successful.

-My level of patience for important things is soaring.

-My ability to let go of things, which really don't matter, has drastically improved.

-The experience of being forced to adapt to change has led to easier adaptation with other things.

-I have refocused on self-care to go the distance with special emphasis on practices to increase my own longevity to be here for as long as possible for my son.

-I have faced the fear of great loss, which I thought I wouldn't be able to live through, and have come out on the other side. I am sad, but stronger.

-I enjoy who I am more. I don't feel the need to impress anyone or apologize for what I am, or what I'm not. I have seen what is important and this just isn't.

-I have learned the hard way self-care is the only way to be able to be a caregiver. If I don't take care of me first, I can't take care of anyone else. It is like when you are on an airplane and they tell you to place your own oxygen mask on before helping anyone else. You can't help others if you have no oxygen (This one is SO HARD for me!).

There's more, but the most important takeaway is I got through it and I CAME OUT THE OTHER SIDE. I came out better. I came out stronger. I genuinely like myself more.

If you have to go through something hellish, at least you can know you will come out on the other side, most likely stronger and better. You may not feel like you will come out on the other side right now, but you will. I promise.

Originally published on the blog, livingthespecialneedslife.com on 2/21/19

WHY STREAMLINING IS IMPORTANT WHEN LIVING THE SPECIAL NEEDS LIFE – OR, WHY ALL OF MY SOCKS ARE EXACTLY THE SAME

Every single sock I own is exactly the same. OK, that's not entirely true. I have two pairs of trouser socks (for business meetings) I never wear anymore since I became a stay-at-home mom. I keep thinking that if I get rid of them, a meeting will come along and I would need to wear them. Since I never want to attend a meeting again where I would have to wear trouser socks, by owning them, I feel as though I am somehow warding off those meetings.

But I digress.

Coming back to the point – ALMOST all of my socks are exactly the same. They are black ankle socks. They are the same brand. I probably own 15 or 20 pairs but I never, ever have to pair them. Because if they are exactly the same, why bother? I can just grab ANY two socks and I have a matching pair.

Imagine a life where you never have to match your socks again. Think of the minutes you would save over the course of your lifetime, never having to wonder if there really is a sock monster eating your socks in the dryer. Sounds good, doesn't it?

This is called streamlining. It works. You should try it. Here's why.

When you are living the special needs life, it is so easy to get bogged down in details. Getting ready to leave the house can be like packing for a long trip to a vacation spot you never quite get to. My son, Kai, just turned seven and it still feels this way. Kai has cognitive disabilities but needs no physical assistive accessories. Still, we have a diaper bag. In the diaper bag we usually have diapers, wipes, a changing towel (because we have long outgrown changing tables), baby food, spoons, a bowl, a sippy cup, two changes of clothes, cookies, two tablets and a hot spot, grocery bags for soiled diapers and clothes, any medications Kai may need, and usually more. Now, if your child has physical disabilities, on top of this could be added a wheelchair, assistive technology for communication, crutches, J-tube or J-Tube accessories and many, many more things. Parents of typical children fondly remember how much stuff they packed when their kids were newborns. To special needs parents and caregivers, a newborn diaper bag seems like a cakewalk.

Assuming we finally have it all together and our child is ready to leave the house, the bottom line is we still have to get ourselves ready, too. Why would I want to search for two socks that match?

Think this sock thing is ridiculous? Let's try another example.

How many times a day does your child with special needs have accidents and need a change of clothes? Oh, but wait, the bedding got wet, too. And then at lunch, food was dropped all over their shirt (if you are lucky and it's just the shirt). All of this stuff needs to be washed.

Are you still separating whites and colors? Doing different loads in hot, warm, cold, delicate, regular? Guess what? I'm not. EVERYTHING gets washed in cold (unless it's a really, really gross mess). EVERYTHING gets washed together. Colors and whites are united in a vat of lovely cold water. Got delicates? Wash ALL of it on the delicate cycle. It comes out exactly the same. I promise.

Streamline. Simplify. Make the process easier. Go with your natural hair texture most of the time. That's right, put the flat iron down. Want to work out? Save money and time by doing it outside or at home online. You never have to worry about gym hours or gym bills. Are you the cook in the house? Make a big pot of some type of grain (rice, pasta, etc.) and keep it in the fridge for several days. It's a quick way to make meals, just change up add-ons and sauce. Doing Keto? Keep the concept, switch the grain to a batch of chicken. Keep it easy. Making pancakes for your kid on Sunday morning? Make extra, slide into Ziplock bags with wax paper in between and you have more meals for the week.

Make your morning routine simpler by laying out everything the night before (yes, I am becoming my mother – not a bad thing). Then, in the morning, instead of spending a few extra minutes trying to find things, you can spend a few extra minutes lingering over coffee. Or, you know, spending time with your kid.

Speaking of your kid, you know that diaper bag I talked about earlier? How many times have you left the house with what you thought was everything only to discover one really important thing was not replaced the last time it was used? MAKE A CHECKLIST. It is impossible to keep everything you need to remember in your brain when living the special needs life. The diaper bag checklist makes the process faster, easier and more complete. When you go to replenish supplies in the diaper bag, look at the list. Go down it and check to make sure everything on the list is in the bag. Done. No brain gymnastics required.

These are just ideas. Streamlining will look different for everyone because everyone is different. What we all have in common as special needs caregivers is being on overload. All of the time. So, streamline. Simplify as much as you can. Make the process as easy as possible.

You deserve easy.

Originally published on the blog, livingthespecialneedslife.com on 2/25/19

A SETBACK DOESN'T HAVE TO BE A DOWNFALL

I hurt my knee. It sucks because I have this ongoing goal – I want to be able to pick up my son and carry him for as long as I possibly can. You see, even though he is seven, he has eight different special needs diagnoses. Developmentally he is about 1 1/2-2 years old. He loves to be held and carried and loved on. As his Mommy, I love to do this, but it kept getting harder as he grew. So I decided to get in better shape.

I know when you begin to get in shape, you need to start where you are. Last fall, I started walking for fifteen minutes a day. This was where I was, after a few rough years where the last thing I felt I had time for was to take care of myself (I was SO wrong, but that discussion is in another chapter). My ability level was low, my weight was high, my exhaustion level was higher. But this new goal, to do this for my son, was unlike any other goal I had ever had before. It wasn't about fitting into a pair of jeans. Or looking pretty/sexy/normal/whatever. It was for my boy, the most important person in my world. For him, I would and will do anything. I decided to do this.

After several months of walking, I was able to walk for almost two hours a day. Just walk. No swinging arms, no speedy hips, no fancy moves. I added in light weight lifting, but I wanted more direction. I hired a trainer who just so happens to own her own CrossFit gym. After working out with her for a couple of months, I decided to go for it. I went to a CrossFit class.

CrossFit, to me, had a pretty high intimidation factor. It is almost a status symbol when you do CrossFit. It is pictured in social media as a brutal workout, done by those crazy gym rats. You know the ones – protein shake chugging, rep discussing, intimidating as hell ripped bodies. I don't think I would have even considered it except my trainer was so phenomenal, I knew she wouldn't recommend it to me if she didn't think I could do it.

Guess what? I can do it. And so can you.

If you think for one second the intimidation factor of entering a CrossFit gym is even CLOSE to what you have experienced as the parent/caregiver of a special needs child, you are wrong. Nope. Not even close. Remember the deer in the headlights, stomach sinking feeling when you found out your child was different? That you were now in charge of someone who needed help with ADHD/Autism/

PVL/CP/a trach tube/Extra Chromosomes/Not Enough Chromosomes/fill in the blank with your chosen term here?

I walked in. I felt the fear, the intimidation and I did it. I LOVED it. And believe me, if I can do it, anyone can.

I can pick up my son. I have to keep going, though, and one day I will lose this game, because he will simply outgrow me. But not yet. Not yet.

There is a fear of getting hurt. Of having a setback. And when you are on the path and you've got everything going and things are humming along, setbacks suck.

I hurt my knee yesterday. I have class tomorrow. I REALLY want to go but...my knee.

It makes me think of when my son has a setback. Does your child have them too? Does your child forget what they have learned over a school break? Does your child start to speak and then stop, having to relearn how to say things over and over again? Do they totally get a concept one day, only to lose it on another? Or can they do certain physical movements sometimes and not at all at other times? Eat without choking on Monday but choke on everything on Thursday?

What do we do when this happens? Do we quit? Nah. WE DON'T HAVE THAT OPTION. We take a break, we rest, we regroup. And we try again. And again. Because this is our CHILD that we are talking about. There is no choice but to keep going.

So why do we give up on ourselves?

Why do we stop taking care of ourselves?

People are scared to get hurt. Look, no one likes to get hurt. I hate it. I am limping around the house, using ice and ibuprofen and a knee brace. I am in pain, stiff and irritable. But, what if last fall, I never started from fear of the unknown? Fear of getting hurt?

Setbacks suck. But you know what sucks more? Not coming back from a setback. This goes for your health, your emotional state, your monetary situation, your relationship woes, everything.

Without a doubt, YOU WILL HAVE SETBACKS IN YOUR LIFE. And, of course, your child with special needs will as well. This is unavoidable. But you know what IS avoidable? A setback becoming a downfall.

Tomorrow I will limp into CrossFit. And, as my lower body heals, I will do what will probably be a challenging all upper body workout.

Rest. Regroup. Return. Someone incredibly important is counting on you.

Originally published on the blog, livingthespecialneedslife.com on 10/2/19

THIS IS THE GREATEST TIME IN HISTORY FOR YOUR CHILD WITH SPECIAL NEEDS TO BE ALIVE

To say that Texas is like its own country is not an overstatement. One of the things I really had to adjust to as a new Texan, having been raised in New York and lived in Los Angeles and Las Vegas, is that Texas moves along in time at its own pace. And, sometimes, depending on the topic or cultural perspective, they are about 20 or more years behind those other places.

For example, when I first became a teacher in Texas, I noticed the staff was multicultural, but they seated themselves in a segregated manner at staff meetings. The Black folk sat with the Black folk. The Hispanic folk formed their own group. The white folks tended to be in their own space as well. There were no Asian folk at all. Having grown up as a minority, a white-looking woman in a Black neighborhood, this was WAY outside my comfort zone.

In New York, just from a practical standpoint, there is not enough space to do this. In a city of more than 8 million people on an island 13 miles by 2 miles, people get used to mixing. That's not to say it is always peaceful, but often, it is.

We moved last year from Fort Worth to a tiny town in East Texas. In some ways, it was like moving even further back in time. The town is quaint, the folks know each other. There is a Main Street of businesses. The other day I went to the Wal-Mart in town and saw a couple decked out from head to toe in camo, and it was not a fashion statement. They were getting ready to go hunting. Behind them, about 20 feet back, I saw a guy in a huge cowboy hat, Wrangler jeans and boots. This is everyday life here. It is wildly different from New York.

It took a long time to get used to Texas.

What stands out to me, incredibly, is the one area in which my tiny town in East Texas exceeds my experiences. This is in the area of special needs acceptance. They not only exceed any other place I have lived, they blow those places out of the water.

My son, who has special needs, goes to a completely special needs dedicated campus. While many students need and have inclusion in the general education setting, my son is low functioning so this is not and never will be appropriate for him. The campus does a stellar job, loves all of their special needs students and they are team players.

This has not, to put it mildly, been my experience in other places I have lived.

My neurotypical eight-year-old daughter goes to regular public school. She is in her second year in a row sharing her class with a kid who is autistic. The school has created such an accepting and warm environment it is a normal occurrence to hear students from different grades greeting this child in the halls. His classmates accept him totally. Any "strange" behavior is merely accepted as *his* normal. These children are 7-10 years old. And THIS IS THEIR NORMAL.

This same daughter is in a karate class in East Texas. This class accommodates students with a wide variety of special needs. My son does not attend because I don't believe he is developmentally ready but he could and might in the future. I recently participated in a Facebook discussion created by the Sensei (teacher). He asked, "If you were to have a tournament and include a special needs division, what are some names we could call that division?" No fewer than FIFTY people participated in the discussion! Although there were some who obviously "didn't get it" when it came to being sensitive about what to call the division, everyone seemed to see the importance of having that division and honoring it.

Think back to the 1900s (not so long ago). Special needs children were often institutionalized. They didn't go to school. They were called names like "retard." They were fringe people. They were picked on. And much, much worse.

You can say whatever you want about the current political climate. About the changes in our country in the last couple of years. But I will say this with absolute certainty: When a karate dojo in rural America has a special needs division and wants to give it a special name to honor special needs folk, our society has achieved greatness. When rural elementary children accept children with special needs as peers, we have arrived where we should be. At least in this area.

I am comforted. For my son, and all our amazing special needs angels. This is the greatest time in history for them to be alive.

Originally published on the blog, livingthespecialneedslife.com on 12/1/18

AFTERWARD

I am honored you took the time to read this book. It is my privilege to walk the walk with all of the amazing special needs folk and their caregivers in our world-wide community. I learn more from you every single day and am so grateful.

I invite you to please check out my blog, livingthespecialneedslife.com and sign up to receive e-mail notifications when there is a new blog post. Currently there are over 125 different topics posted.

If you would like to contact me, I would love to hear from you. Please send me an e-mail at livingthespecialneedslife@gmail.com.

If you purchased this book, on behalf of my son, Kai, I would like to thank you. Money from the sale of this book goes toward equestrian therapy sessions for Kai and other caregiving essentials.

HOW YOU CAN HELP

Thank you for reading! Hopefully this book will help you on your joyful journey with your special needs child. You've already done so much, just by purchasing this book, to help you move forward in a siutuation you probably didn't expect to find yourself in.

Now that you're finished, though, there's one more thing you can do: You can help other people in the same situation you were!

Please take a moment to **review this book** on whatever social media site you use or wherever you purchased this copy. Reviews let other people know what you thought and how it can help them. Additionally, the more reviews a book gets, the higher it moves in the algorithms to show it to anyone who might be looking for something similar.

I thank you, from the bottom of my heart, for helping me spread the word.

ABOUT THE AUTHOR

Mara spent fifteen years teaching general education from pre-K through second grade before staying home to care for her son Kai, who has special needs. She is certified to teach both general and special needs education as well as ESL (English as a Second Language).

Mara is a Step-Mom, a Birth-Mom and a Special Needs Mom. Her children, children-in-law and grandchildren include Autum, Ace, Summer, Amaya, Kai, Jason, Meagan, Austin, Jacob, Riley, Thea, and Zoey. Mara currently lives in the woods in East Texas with her awesome partner in crime, her husband Billy.

Want more caregiving content? Check out her blog, livingthespecialneedslife.com.

www.ingramcontent.com/pod-product-compliance
Lightning Source LLC
LaVergne TN
LVHW051524070426
835507LV00023B/3293